STANWOOD Shot Dead!

Death, Diplomacy, and the Dawn of American Power

Nick Pietrowicz

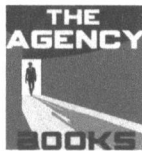

THE AGENCY BOOKS

an imprint of Sunbury Press, Inc.
Mechanicsburg, PA USA

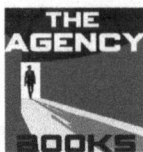

THE AGENCY BOOKS

an imprint of Sunbury Press, Inc.
Mechanicsburg, PA USA

For information about special discounts for bulk purchases, please contact Sunbury Press Orders Dept. at (855) 338-8359 or orders@sunburypress.com.

To request one of our authors for speaking engagements or book signings, please contact Sunbury Press Publicity Dept. at publicity@sunburypress.com.

FIRST AGENCY BOOKS EDITION: June 2025

Set in Adobe Garamond Pro | Interior design by Crystal Devine | Cover by Lawrence Knorr | Edited by Sarah Peachey.

Publisher's Cataloging-in-Publication Data
Names: Pietrowicz, Nick, author.
Title: Stanwood shot dead! / Nick Pietrowicz.
Description: First trade paperback edition. | Mechanicsburg, PA : The Agency Books, 2025.
Summary: *Stanwood shot dead! death, diplomacy, and the dawn of American power* relates the true story of adventurer Louis Duverge and his killing of American consular agent Victor Stanwood in 1888 Madagascar. Duverge's scandalous life as a mercenary, Civil War officer, American diplomat, and African explorer frames this forgotten nineteenth-century mystery.
Identifiers: ISBN : 979-8-88819-324-2 (paperback).
Subjects: HISTORY / General | HISTORY / United States / Civil War Period (1850–1877) | International Relations / Diplomacy.

Designed in the USA
0 1 1 2 3 5 8 13 21 34 55

For the Love of Books!

For Stefan and Alexandra,
my two favorite diplomats

Contents

Preface

At the entrance to the State Department, there is a memorial for diplomats who died while serving abroad. On that sacred wall are the names, dates, locations, and manners of death of more than 320 men and women. One day, for no particular reason, I stopped to look at the memorial and noticed the name Victor F. W. Stanwood. Next to it was written: "Murdered." It was a highly unusual death among a list of unusual deaths. Stanwood's nineteenth-century companions on the wall had died from "Exposure," "Dysentery," "African Fever," and "Volcanic Eruption," or were "Lost at Sea." Death by trauma and disease was common, but murders were rare. Curious, I pulled out my phone and searched his name. The official American Foreign Service Association (AFSA) record of Stanwood, the organization that maintains the solemn memorial, stated that his murder was related to his attempts to end the slave trade in Madagascar. Now I was more curious. The wall indicated that Stanwood had died in 1888. The transatlantic slave trade had ended over two decades before. Which enslavers was he fighting during a time when American diplomacy was more focused on commerce than correcting misbehavior in other countries? The name of his killer was listed. I googled him. A ship captain named Duverge—he had shot Stanwood during a dispute about a vessel. Perhaps the slavery angle was merely tagged onto a less exciting death to make Stanwood's legacy more appealing, I thought. I made a note to check later and went about my work inside the State Department.

But I soon forgot about Stanwood and Duverge. I am a special agent with the State Department's Diplomatic Security Service. My agency protects American diplomats around the world, and while the work is exciting and gratifying, it is also constant and occasionally overwhelming. I cannot remember the crisis that prevented me from pursuing my initial interest in Stanwood's death. I seem to remember a coup attempt someplace in the tropics. Or maybe a kidnapping in Eastern Europe. Diplomatic Security secures more than 250 American embassies and consulates, and while each crisis is handled with tremendous seriousness, once finished, there is a tendency to move quickly on to the next danger. That pattern tends to promote forgetfulness. Regardless of the reason, I was drawn away from the mystery for several months. When I eventually walked by the wall again and again noticed Stanwood's name and place and manner of death, I was reminded of my earlier question: Had he really died because he was fighting slavery?

I set aside some time to research Stanwood and his murderer. The three or four accounts I located online recited essentially the same information as the AFSA record, with minor additions. Stanwood had been fighting enslavers, particularly their misuse of the American flag at sea. Duverge was the captain of a schooner, the *Solitaire*. The vessel had somehow grounded in Madagascar, and he and Stanwood disputed what was to be done next. One night, their dispute became heated, and Duverge shot the consular agent dead. Now more curious, I searched the original consular messages (so-called "despatches") for answers. I was stunned when I discovered that Duverge was a former American consular official. I had been a DSS agent for twenty years; I believed I knew every major criminal incident in the history of the State Department. Yet I had never heard of this killing of a diplomat by another American diplomat. Upon reflection, I realized that most of my knowledge of diplomatic security began with the early twentieth century, when the modern Foreign Service emerged. Of violent crimes against diplomats before that time, I realized, I knew very little. Perhaps learning more from that period could illuminate my understanding of today. I expanded my search outside of State Department records.

The National Archives contained thorough records of diplomatic correspondence surrounding the matter, and newspapers from the time gave hints of Stanwood and his alleged killer. Duverge, it seemed, was actually a French baron. Archives in France provided more details. He was also an officer in the American Civil War. Diaries and histories from his unit gave glimpses of his service during the war. He was a ship captain. Admiralty records outlined his time at sea, both in America and abroad. Documents from Madagascar indicated that Stanwood, too, had been a sailor before settling on the island as a merchant. But it was Duverge's history, riddled with immorality, that was most fascinating. He was a habitual adulterer and liar, as well as a suspected slave trader, arms dealer, deserter, mutineer, rapist, and murderer. Duverge was not a good man, but he was a man who had seen a good deal of the world. He could sail, ride, shoot, and drink as well as anyone, and he would fight any man who challenged him on it. Here was the story of an actual Victorian-era scoundrel whose life of ill repute culminated in the murder of an American diplomat.

Piecing it together required records from Washington, New York, London, Mauritius, Paris, Sydney, Brussels, Antananarivo, Charleston, and other places, each one bringing new light to the crimes of Duverge and the sad ending of Victor Stanwood. I have annotated the text with citations to these sources. The consular despatches that constitute much of the historical record surrounding Stanwood's death and Duverge's adventures in Angola and Madagascar are almost entirely complete and available online from the National Archives. Where I have quoted a despatch but cited a different source, it is because the original record is missing or illegible. Place names used are those that were common during the latter half of the nineteenth century, unless otherwise noted. Duverge's name at birth was Louis Leopold Du Rothier Du Verge. I have generally used the most common Anglicized spelling, "Louis Duverge."

Sources originally written in French or Portuguese, I translated myself. For Malagasy translations, and his scrupulous research of the Archives of the Republic of Madagascar in Antananarivo, I am grateful to Bako Narahintsoa. He is one of many who were kind enough to assist me with this work. I must also thank David A. Langbart of the National Archives in Washington; Graham Grist and Dr. Graham Neale of the Orders and Medals Research Society; Jim McCarthy and Christopher Shea of Gallaudet University; Wayne Compton of the New York City Episcopalian Archives; Wade Dorsey of the South Carolina State Archives; Father David J. Endres of Mount St. Mary's Seminary and School of Theology; William Kurtz, formerly of the John L. Nau III Center for Civil War History at the University of Virginia; Meaghan Wright of the Peabody Essex Museum; LTC Matthew Sousa, U.S. Army; Professor Gwyn Campbell of McGill University; Professor Jennifer Cole of the University of Chicago; Caroline Seagle of the Indian Ocean World Centre; Alan Silverleib of Harvard University; Agnes Sandras of the Bibliothèque nationale de France; Professor Solofo Randrianja of Toamasina; and Alston Richardson, Jean Pierre Montocchio, and Dr. Mathilde Leduc of the Royal Museum for Central Africa, Brussels. Without their help, Stanwood and Duverge's story would remain forgotten.

CHAPTER ONE

Our Men in Madagascar

On December 21, 1888, the State Department received a cable from the American Consulate in Madagascar. The message, written in the succinct, staccato fashion of telegrams from that age, announced, "Consular Agent Stanwood shot dead at Belo South of Andakabe November fifth by Captain Duverge of Schooner Solitaire."[1]

Victor F. W. Stanwood was the fifth American diplomat to die by homicide. The first, U.S. consul Harris E. Fudger, was killed in 1825 in Bogota, Colombia, after a competing suitor impaled him with a sword. Henrikus Heusken, an interpreter at the newly established consulate in Edo, Japan, was cut down in 1861 by political radicals. A year later, William Baker, a consul in Mexico, was murdered by Apaches. Henry Sawyer, the consul in Paramaribo, Suriname, was killed by a sailor in 1877. Of these, only Heusken's murder, which initiated a serious diplomatic conflict between the United States and Japan, resulted in significant attention back in Washington.

Stanwood's murder, though not political, provoked similar interest. America's involvement around the world had grown considerably in the final quarter of the nineteenth century, and it was important that the matter be handled properly for an aspiring power. Both the White House and Congress demanded answers about the tragedy. Officials at the State Department scrambled to collect information from far-off Madagascar while also pondering what to do about Stanwood's alleged murderer, who had fled to the island's interior. The killing also generated news outside of Washington. Most major American newspapers published stories about Stanwood and the subsequent trial of his accused murderer. Reports of a diplomat shot down in an exotic locale and news about his mysterious killer sold papers, at least for a few months. But ultimately, the story, like official interest in Stanwood's death, faded away.

In 1933, the American Foreign Service Association installed a memorial plaque at the entrance of what is now the Eisenhower Executive Office Building, next to the White House. The plaque commemorated American diplomats who died in the line of duty. Stanwood's name was included. The press release that accompanied the memorial unveiling improperly gave Andakabe, Stanwood's duty station, as his place of death instead of Belo. No one seemed to notice the error, though; Stanwood's death by then was nearly half a century in the past. When the State Department relocated to its current headquarters in Foggy Bottom, the plaque was moved as well. As more and more names were added, Stanwood's sad end slipped further into history, as did the names of those who were involved in the events that led to his death. But Victor Stanwood and the circumstances surrounding his murder are worth revisiting.

Stanwood was a consular agent, subordinate to the U.S. consul in Tamatave. Tamatave, the country's major port, was located in the northeast of Madagascar. Part clerk, part banker, part judge, sometimes intelligence officer, and occasional ambassador, an American consul in the nineteenth century fulfilled the role of the federal government in places that were often weeks away from direct contact with Washington. There was no shortage of work. Consuls issued passports, received mail, cashed checks, and provided credit on behalf of American citizens abroad. When a citizen was born or died overseas, consuls dutifully recorded the event and transmitted a formal record to the State Department. Consular officers in the late 1800s could even serve in a judicial capacity, holding civil or criminal trials to determine liability or guilt in disputes between Americans. Stanwood's primary duty, though, was to promote trade. When a ship from the United States arrived in Morondava, the port adjacent to Andakabe, Stanwood assisted the vessel in complying with the terms of an 1867 treaty of commerce and 1881 treaty of friendship between Madagascar and the United States. He maintained contact with the U.S. consul in Tamatave and Washington via the diplomatic pouch, a system which allowed for slow but supposedly confidential communication.

Stanwood's work was part of a consular tradition that originated in Egypt more than two millennia before, where Greek states had established magisterial offices along the Lower Nile. These courts provided Hellenic merchants with an avenue for legal relief outside the Egyptian system. During the first century A.D., Rome sent representatives abroad to assist its citizens engaged in trade. After the fall of the Empire, these agents disappeared. But with the rise of Mediterranean trading states in the eleventh century and the establishment of the Hanseatic League in the late twelfth century, a need for functionaries in cities across the region again emerged. The title of "consul" came into use during this period despite the modern position having little connection to the elected office in the Roman Republic. These officials were effective in smoothing over disputes between their citizens abroad, helping to encourage trade that enriched their own countries and the locations where they served. Consuls were soon deployed from London to Lviv to Lisbon. Their work was distinct from that of ambassadors, who represented the interests of their governments to foreign states. Ambassadors had existed as long as consuls but, until the thirteenth century, were usually only appointed for a fixed period—such as the duration of an alliance or to resolve a specific dispute. As the interests of European states became more interwoven, the need for ambassadors increased. It became common for ambassadors to be assigned to foreign capitals and courts indefinitely as opposed to merely embarking on a specific mission and then returning to their home country.[2] Thus developed the two separate tracts of foreign representation that continue to exist today: consular and ambassadorial. Ambassadors promoted a state's political goals, while their consular counterparts helped citizens in need of governmental services abroad.

A consul's work, sometimes intentionally, sometimes not, often strayed into the area of political influence. French consuls in America in the late 1700s were present to assist French citizens, but also served to inform Paris that the colonies seemed worthy of assistance. Even American consuls during this period exercised political influence, albeit indirectly. Midway through the American Revolution, Congress appointed America's first consul, Lieutenant Colonel William Palfrey, to Paris to improve commerce with France and thereby enhance political relations.[3] Congress's second appointment was a consular agent to Havana. The

Spanish ambassador to the United States later estimated that commerce facilitated by American consuls did more to protect Cuba from British or French interference than any negotiations between Madrid and Washington.[4] By 1800, more than fifty American consular posts were present throughout Europe, the Caribbean, and North Africa.

The Founders formalized the importance of diplomats of all forms in Article 2, Section 2 of the Constitution. Therein, the president is granted the authority to appoint, with the advice and consent of the Senate, "ambassadors, ministers and consuls." Until 1924, when President Coolidge signed the Rogers Act, commonly known as the Foreign Service Act, the United States maintained two separate branches of overseas representation: the consular service and the diplomatic service. The diplomatic service, led in a foreign country by an ambassador, was America's formal political representation abroad. Ambassadors and their staff negotiated agreements with foreign states, reported on the political developments of their host country, represented the United States during important ceremonies, and served as the plenary authority for official American interests in their assigned country. The consular service promoted American commerce and provided governmental services to citizens abroad. The consular service continued its growth throughout the nineteenth century. By the time of Stanwood's appointment to Madagascar in October 1881, the State Department maintained more than three hundred consular posts.

The American consulate in Tamatave (today called "Toamasina") was headed, at the time of Stanwood's appointment, by Consul William W. Robinson. Robinson, a veteran of the Mexican-American War and Civil War, oversaw Tamatave-based Vice-Consul Roger Whitney and two consular agency posts. Robert Andrew was America's consular agent in Majunga (today Mahajanga) on Madagascar's northwest coast. Victor Stanwood served in Andakabe (today a neighborhood of what was then the nearby town of Morondava) on Madagascar's southwest coast. While J. A. Poupard, an Englishman, served as Robinson's secretary, his vice-consul and both consular agents were U.S. citizens.[5] There was no American diplomat in 1881 in Antananarivo, Madagascar's capital and largest city. Consul Robinson's Tamatave consulate was something of a sore point with Malagasy authorities, who aimed to relocate all foreign officials to the capital in order to highlight the legitimacy of their rule. This was part of a larger initiative to emphasize the country's autonomy in the face of pressure from potential European colonization. That effort was ineffective. The major powers preferred to keep their representatives in Tamatave. In this sense, Robinson's status as a consul and not an ambassador was beneficial. Whereas other foreign representatives struggled to explain to their Malagasy hosts why they seated their ambassadors away from the court in Antananarivo, Robinson could rightfully argue that he was situated in Tamatave to best serve Americans visiting the country's largest port. At the same time, as he admitted discreetly in a letter to President Cleveland, "So long as we have no diplomatic representation near this government a large portion of the Consul's duties must be quasi diplomatic—it cannot be avoided—by reason of the distance from Washington, and long time required to write for and get special instructions, he is and must be compelled to act without them except upon the most important matters."[6]

The Malagasies had good reason to worry about outside intrusions. From its discovery, the island had offered a tempting target for adventurers from abroad.

The earliest settlers in Madagascar likely arrived between the fourth and fifth centuries A.D. from an unknown location in maritime Southeast Asia. Over the following two or three centuries, inhabitants from mainland Africa relocated to Madagascar. Arab traders concurrently established rudimentary trading settlements along its coasts. Portuguese explorers commenced limited commerce with the native population in the sixteenth century. In the late seventeenth century, French trade with the island began and, soon after, the English appeared. As curious outsiders visited Madagascar's shores, tribal groups battled for control of the island's interior. For centuries, no single clan could secure dominance over the other groups. The arrival of the English tipped the balance in favor of the Imerina tribe. In exchange for ending the export of slaves, London granted the Merina, as they came to be styled by the British, military and other assistance. The Merina ruled through a caste system that severely restricted mobility between classes. The population was divided into nobility, aristocrats, commoners, and slaves. The commoners, known as the Hova, constituted the mass of the Merina army.

By the early 1800s, the Merina tribe, believed to be originally a coastal people, ruled most of the central plains of Madagascar from their capital, Antananarivo. Merina control over Madagascar, including ending the slave trade, was not complete. The island's west coast remained in the hands of other groups, principally the Sakalava tribes. The Sakalava, with access to wealth and weapons from Arab merchants, resisted Merina domination. Gradually, they aligned themselves with the French, who offered assistance to counter the Merina as a check against the British. The British-Merina alliance was unsteady. While the Merina welcomed English firearms and military advisors, they were less enthusiastic about British missionaries. Those interlopers and other European evangelicals threatened the complex class structures that fortified Merina rule.

The infamous Queen Ranavalona I's rise to the throne in 1828 marked a pushback against all European influence, including that of the British. She ejected most foreigners and prohibited the practice of Christianity. Simultaneously, she violently sought to assert her authority outside Madagascar's central plains, attacking regional tribal rulers who failed to submit entirely to Merina subjugation. Ranavalona directed her wrath in particular against the Sakalava. It is likely that over a million of the island's inhabitants were killed under Ranavalona's orders, yet she never fully secured the island for the Merina, who, by this time, were increasingly being referred to as "Hovas."[7] Consul Robinson informed Washington that "the Sakalava tribes stand in similar relation to the Hovas and the Queen's government, to that of our indians [sic] to our people and government."[8] Against this internal pressure was the ever-present threat of European conquest. Ranavalona balanced a justifiable concern about foreign meddling with a need for outside expertise. While most foreigners were expelled, a select few were permitted to remain and advise the Hovas on modernization attempts. Among these was Joseph-François Lambert, a French slave trader who negotiated a surreptitious agreement with Ranavalona's son, granting Lambert significant natural resource concessions in Madagascar. Following an aborted coup attempt by Lambert, he was banished from the island, departing for Mauritius in 1858. Three years later, the queen died and Lambert returned. Finding his old friend the prince well disposed to their earlier agreement, Lambert set about establishing a lucrative business in mining and agriculture. The terms of the so-called Lambert Charter included Lambert's company's right to acquire title to real property, a hitherto unheard-of allowance in Malagasy law. Following a series of government changes and disputes with Lambert and the administrators of his company, the Government of France insisted upon full application of the charter.[9] This was one of several pretexts used by the French to justify their invasion of Madagascar and the first French-Hova War of 1883–1886.

French aspirations in Madagascar were hardly a surprise. Throughout the nineteenth century, astute Malagasy leaders had attempted to counter French expansionism using diplomatic and public appeals. During the 1870s and 1880s, representatives from Madagascar embarked on missions to European capitals and Washington, seeking support for their country's continued independence. At one point, American Consul Robinson temporarily left his official posting in Tamatave to accompany Hova diplomats to Europe and America, where he advocated for the Malagasy cause. The State Department permitted this unusual effort, conditional upon Robinson's assurances that he would make it clear to foreign officials that he was acting in his personal capacity. These diplomatic exercises were especially fruitful in London, where British missionaries feared French Catholic advances on the island. During an era where Dr. David Livingstone had electrified evangelical zeal in his home country, the Malagasy's diplomats found no shortage of supporters in the United Kingdom. Whitehall was also interested in Madagascar, noting the opportunity to hinder French influence in southern Africa and perhaps expand opportunities for British merchants. The interests of the United States were less meddlesome than the European powers. American consuls courteously communicated messages of support from Washington to the throne in Antananarivo, but mostly promoted trade in Madagascar. Advice was given about what goods might be imported from Boston or New York for the mutual benefit of both countries. Madagascar's appeal to potential European conquerors, however, was apparent to Consul Robinson. Writing to Washington soon after his arrival in Madagascar in 1875, he characterized the Hova government's impossible dilemma: "England or France, or perhaps both, will, soon or later, make as excuse, some question of dispute or matter of outrage . . . and seize the island."[10]

France and the United Kingdom sought to gain Washington's support for their ambitions in Madagascar. An 1883 visit to the United States by Malagasy diplomats included two Englishmen quietly embedded with the Hova government, ostensibly to assist with modernizing Madagascar's diplomatic corps but actually to promote London's interests. The French might very well have sent their own agents to America to counter British claims to Madagascar. An anonymous pamphlet published in New York concurrent with the 1883 visit emphasized that Americans should "steer clear from the quarrel of the English and French disputants." Notably, the publisher of this pamphlet, one "Thompson and Moreau Printers," specialized in translating and republishing European works, predominantly from France, into American English. While it is unknown if the text was an instrument of the French government, it certainly served as a means of propaganda for the French cause in Madagascar.[11]

The Malagasies valued America's position of neutrality in the conflict. In 1884, Consular Agent Stanwood appeared in the Malagasy press for the first time following his return to Andakabe via a rarely traveled route from Antananarivo. The *Madagascar Times* applauded the journey, noting that while the French and English were busy "quarreling," Stanwood's travels were designed to help "American merchants understand that there is unbounded wealth in this island." Malagasies appreciated that American interests were focused on commerce, not conquest. While America never forced Antananarivo to act in a certain manner, it did humbly suggest one reform. Following the conclusion of the American Civil War, Washington joined the European powers in encouraging Madagascar to ban not just the export of slaves but the institution of slavery entirely. In 1887, Antananarivo agreed and, at least in a legal sense, slavery in all its evil forms was ended on the island.

In this complex environment of foreign intrigue and internal drama, America's consular representatives in Madagascar carried out their work. Consular despatches, reports from post to Washington, show Tamatave to be mostly a port of potential. Occasional visits from American vessels created some work for Consul Robinson and Vice-Consul Whitney, but much of the time the two were left free to draft reports about the need for American goods, and possibilities for future commerce. Consular Agent Andrew in Majunga enjoyed a similarly slow-paced assignment.

Madagascar's central west coast, though, was a different matter. The Hova had never established complete control of this region, and it remained a lawless safe haven for smugglers, pirates, criminals, deserters, and all forms of late nineteenth-century outlaws. Immediately after his appointment to Andakabe, Stanwood penned a series of letters to Robinson detailing continuous violations of the 1867 treaty between the United States and Madagascar by "American" vessels.[12] Under that agreement, the United States was granted permission to station consuls in Malagasy ports. In exchange, the consuls were to endeavor to compel American captains to pay proper customs duties and adhere to local and international laws. Stanwood's communiques complained of rampant misuse of the American flag by slave trading vessels, which were only very rarely, if ever, American. Knowing that the British naval vessels that regularly patrolled the Mozambique Channel between Madagascar and continental Africa would not board a vessel flying the Stars and Stripes, slave traders improperly hoisted the American flag for protection. This practice was "unofficially encouraged by French authorities to facilitate the supply of labour to their plantation colonies."[13] Stanwood recorded American transgressions as well. Andakabe was hardly Liverpool or Le Havre. When ships from Boston and other American ports appeared in Madagascar, Stanwood took notice. And when these ships arrived full of goods, yet returned to America without reporting any official cargo, Stanwood took more than notice. He investigated these peculiar visits and assessed that many American vessels were in Madagascar for illegal trade. Stanwood contended that American merchants were supplying powder and firearms to Sakalava chiefs, possibly in exchange for slaves to be sold elsewhere in the region. He sent missives to Consul Robinson in Tamatave, demanding that something be done.

Stanwood's writings to Robinson were usually tabled. Only occasionally did Robinson see it fit to forward Stanwood's reports to the State Department. At one point, he went over a year without responding. Robinson later claimed Stanwood's reputation as an exaggerator, well-intentioned but prone to hyperbole, justified this decision. Justified or not, Stanwood was not pleased. In a flagrant breach of protocol, Stanwood wrote directly to the State Department about his observations of misuse of the flag and general lawlessness in Madagascar. He also raised the issue of relocating the Tamatave consulate to Antananarivo with Washington, which infuriated Consul Robinson. In June 1883, Stanwood even penned a letter directly to President Chester A. Arthur. He demanded that the United States protest the recent French bombardment and occupation of Tamatave, an issue well outside of Standwood's direct authority. Though displeased, Consul Robinson took a muted approach to this insubordination, likely because there was simply no one readily available to replace Stanwood in the undesirable post of Consular Agent Andakabe. Or perhaps he was just waiting for time to pass. In 1885, Robinson abandoned his Madagascar worries entirely, returning to America and a retirement in Wisconsin.

Robinson was replaced in July 1887 by Consul John P. Campbell. Campbell arrived in Madagascar and set about examining his new post. It was immediately apparent that his consular agent in Andakabe was, at best, an active writer. At worst he was something of a rogue actor. Campbell was more aggressive in his handling of Stanwood than had been his predecessor. In September 1887, he sent a despatch to his superiors in Washington, objecting to Stanwood's continued requests to move the consulate from Tamatave to Antananarivo. Indirectly, though, Campbell raised the consular agent's wider insubordination and fitness for duty:

> Of Mr. Stanwood's character of integrity and truth, I have no personal knowledge. All I know I have learned by report since my arrival here and that is not favorable. The records of the consulate show there have been difficulties with him regarding the irregularities of his official correspondence. I therefore, trust under the circumstances the Department will not hold me responsible for any of the acts of Consular agent Stanwood.[14]

In the year and a half following Campbell's arrival in Madagascar, Stanwood continued to voice his complaints. He wrote about the inaction of the Malagasy government in aiding him with a stranded American vessel, alleged libelous claims against him from a newspaper in Antananarivo, griped about the lack of regular communications from the consulate in Tamatave, and repeatedly raised the abuse of the American flag and landing of illicit goods upon Madagascar's western coast.

Each new message delivered increased pleas for action and a decreased level of decorum. Stanwood included among his grievances Campbell's perceived inattention to the welfare of Americans in Andakabe. Writing on June 7, 1888, the consular agent tossed Victorian-era courtesies aside and declared, "you are the most prominent officer in this case, still you are the only one that has been next to silent in the matter."[15]

One month later, the schooner *Solitaire* from Boston arrived in Andakabe. Onboard were seven crew members, two passengers, and Master Louis Leopold Du Rothier Duverge.

A new problem had arrived in Madagascar.

CHAPTER TWO

Baron Duverge

The arrival of the *Solitaire* was not Louis Duverge's first visit to Madagascar. It was probably his second. Or third. Or perhaps fourth. Records of Duverge's life, discoverable from his own accounts and incidental mentions in histories of the era, are incomplete and, at times, even contradictory. What is established clearly, however, is a man who was always on the move. Such peripateticism was in keeping with Duverge's pedigree.

By his account, Louis Leopold Du Rothier Duverge was born on June 3, 1840, in Port Louis, Mauritius. Duverge's maternal history is not well documented, though some sources suggest his mother was a mulatto born to a French mother and Mauritian native. Duverge's paternal line is better recorded. A great-grandfather, born Pierre Rathier Duverge in Bordeaux in 1746, constituted the most prominent of his ancestors. As a young man, Pierre took a civil servant's position in Louisiana. He remained even after France temporarily surrendered the colony to the Spanish in 1763. In 1764, Pierre married a baker's daughter, and five years later, their son, Rathier Duverge, was born in New Orleans. In 1786, the elder Duverge earned a knighthood and was appointed commissioner general to the "Isle of France," a prosperous colony located approximately seven hundred miles off of Madagascar in the Indian Ocean.

The Duverge family seal

His tenure there lasted just three years, ended by the French Revolution. Pierre died in 1810. The same year, the British, then at war with France, seized the island and renamed it Mauritius. The younger Duverge, Rathier, relocated to Reunion Island, likely in 1814, when it reverted to French control, while Mauritius remained a British possession. As the son of the former Mauritian commissioner general, Rathier enjoyed a sinecure appointment in Reunion for the duration of his life, which ended in 1825. The family likely returned to Mauritius around 1830, when the Orleanists removed King Charles X from power and the value of the Duverge name, which was associated with the now ousted Legitimist Bourbons, diminished in the French territories. At that point, the Duverges would have viewed Mauritius, previously the place from which their family had escaped, as a promising alternative to Reunion.

Rathier's son, Astyanax Duverge, was around twenty-five when he arrived in Mauritius. He likely found it to be a relatively easy transition. While the British controlled Mauritius legally and militarily, most of the European population remained culturally French. Nevertheless, in 1850, Astyanax naturalized as a British subject. Such a conversion was necessary to advance his career in the Mauritian civil service, a field he had entered in keeping with the family tradition. Astyanax had by then two sons. Despite their formal status as British subjects, he raised his boys to be French. The children grew up speaking French, attending Catholic services, and hearing regularly about their aristocratic heritage. As male members of the Duverge line descended from Pierre Duverge, they were entitled to use the title "baron." The youngest, Seide Rathier Duverge, would follow in his paternal ancestor's footsteps of public service and eventually become the chief of customs in Port Louis. The older son was Louis Leopold Du Rothier Duverge, who took a different path.

Duverge inherited the familial instinct for relocation. He appears to have departed Mauritius for France around 1853, when he was thirteen. At varying times later, he claimed to have studied at either Bordeaux or at the École Polytechnique in Paris. Duverge, technically a British subject, joined the French Foreign Legion in 1859. Despite his aristocratic title, he was not made an officer. As an enlisted legionnaire, he participated in the Second Italian War of Independence, fighting against the Austrian Empire. He then joined the Chasseurs d'Afrique, a cavalry unit that drew recruits heavily from current and past French colonies. Duverge later told acquaintances that he fought in Algeria. At some point he left terrestrial service and enlisted in the French Navy. Reportedly Duverge was forced to resign from the naval service following a duel, the first hints of a life that was later defined by misconduct and violence. After the navy, Duverge joined the French Merchant Marine. There, he earned his sailing captain's credentials.[1]

In 1863, Duverge signed on with the schooner *Sphynx* as first mate. Serving with eight others under Captain Puren, Duverge departed Mauritius in April en route to Cochin, on the west coast of India. The *Sphynx* was transporting 3,756 gold coins, a sum worth approximately $2 million in 2025. The gold had been placed onboard the ship in four bags deposited in a case. That case was then nailed shut and hidden under the captain's bed. The money was payment for an earlier shipment of palm oil to Mauritius, received from the Indian firm of Regnaud and Son. Several days after the *Sphynx*'s expected arrival in Cochin, Regnaud and Sons received a telegram from Ceylon:

Though he was actually eighteen years old at the time, for unknown reasons in this 1858 passport, Louis Duverge claimed to be a fifteen-year-old student. National Archives – Republic of France.

From Colombo, from Captain Duverge, schooner *Sphynx*, to Cochin, to A. Regnaud. Arrived off this port on the 8th, short of provisions. Went on shore to purchase. Instructed mate to remain off the port till my return. Vessel gone away, having 3,700 sovereigns on board for you. Think crew must have murdered the mate. Make enquiries on the coast. Telegraph should she arrive, and send me instructions. 18 April, 1863.[2]

The owners were alarmed and cabled back to learn what had become of their captain, as Duverge had been engaged as only the first mate. Duverge communicated to them that he would come to Cochin to explain. Upon arrival a week later, he offered his employers a story that more or less mirrored his earlier unconvincing message. He reported that the *Sphynx* had left Mauritius as planned before stopping at Peros Bahos, an isolated atoll in the Chagos Archipelago, to take on drinking water. Captain Puren had then sailed to Colombo, where he ordered Duverge ashore to purchase supplies. Duverge noted that the *Sphynx*, then less than a day from Cochin, was not wanting for provisions or water at the time of their stopping in Colombo. He offered no further information for Puren's decision to visit Ceylon. Asked why he had claimed to be captain of the missing vessel, Duverge at first denied he had ever said as much. After the official from the telegram office in Colombo confirmed that Duverge had indeed called himself "Captain," Duverge blamed his limited English skills, a tactic he would use throughout his life to attempt to avoid responsibility. Perhaps most troubling was Duverge's claim that the ship's captain had been "murdered." Regnaud opined that as a mariner, Duverge should have known that vessels go lost at sea for many reasons. The decision to invoke murder as the answer to the *Sphynx*'s disappearance, in the opinion of the ship's owners, implicated the first mate.

The local authorities were alerted. Duverge again provided incomplete and misleading answers about the journey of the *Sphynx*, convincing investigators that he was involved in some sort of criminal behavior. His replies were "so replete with improbabilities and contraction" that the magistrate ordered Duverge placed under surveillance. Three days later, he disappeared. Soon after, Regnaud received a letter from Duverge, posted from a town several hundred miles north. The note offered Duverge's confession. Duverge claimed he had conspired with the captain to steal the ship's cargo of gold, his share being 1,200 sovereigns. The loot, claimed Duverge, had been buried earlier in the Chagos Islands. Duverge wrote that he believed the captain had abandoned him in Colombo so he could go back to the Chagos and collect the entirety of the proceeds of their theft. Duverge related that he was going to France "to die." Decades later in Madagascar, delusional and lingering near death from fever, Duverge allegedly told a traveling companion that once, while in "the Seychelles," he had "cheated someone" and "wanted to sink the ship to cover up the deed." Duverge said his crime had been uncovered and that he had been forced to hide inside a French vessel to escape. If accurate, this information gives some clarity to the *Sphynx* mystery.

The following scenario seems most plausible.

Captain Puren, by design or chance, took command of a vessel transporting a wealth of gold between Mauritius and India. He acquired, again either deliberately or by good fortune, the morally weak First Mate Duverge. At some point, the two decided to keep the gold, likely bringing the rest of the crew into their scheme. But rather than abscond with the coins in the *Sphynx* and spend the remainder of their lives as fugitives in some far-flung land, distant from the luxuries they could now afford in Bombay or even Paris, they devised a complex plan that would both award them the gold and preserve their perceived innocence. The *Sphynx* would visit the sparsely uninhabited Chagos Islands, which, along with the Maldives and the Seychelles, are the only destinations between Mauritius and India. There, the crew would hide the coins. The ship would then sail to India. There, the crew would scuttle the *Sphynx* close enough to the coast to both safely reach the shore and demonstrate beyond doubt that the vessel and her cargo had been entirely lost at sea. Of course, once there, the crew and officers would be subject to immediate scrutiny. But the gold being already stashed on a remote island, there would be no physical evidence of their misdeed. Only later, when the insurance claim had been paid and suspicions about the *Sphynx's* true fate forgotten, would the conspirators return to the Chagos to recover their loot.

It was a fairly solid plan, provided no one in the group betrayed anyone else. At some point, though, the scheme changed. Nowhere in the conspiracy was it necessary for the first mate to go ashore in Colombo. Something happened between the time the gold was deposited in the Chagos and when Duverge appeared at the telegraph office that altered the original plan. Chances are it was a falling-out between Duverge and the rest of the crew. As demonstrated during the rest of his life,

Duverge was an incapable officer who frequently lost the support of his men and commanders. He also oscillated wildly between scoundrel and self-appointed moralist. Puren and the others must have grown tired of the disagreeable and capricious first mate, who was either demanding a larger cut or had suddenly determined that their deed was improper, and decided to abandon him. Disembarking him in Cochin was impossible. The ship would need to be sunk before their arrival there. But leaving him in Colombo, 250 miles from the *Sphynx*'s owners, would allow the captain and the others to carry out their scheme as planned. Duverge, meanwhile, would have few choices. While he could potentially expose the conspiracy once he realized he had been abandoned, doing so would render him subject to charges as well. His apparent best option would have been to take the money he had been given to buy the unnecessary supplies and find passage back home to Mauritius from Ceylon. Were Duverge a rational person, he would have followed that course. Duverge would have dismissed the *Sphynx* affair as a loss and moved on to his next adventure. But Duverge, always hot-headed, could not accept that he had been cut out of the plan. Instead, he telegraphed the ship's owners in vengeance, hoping the *Sphynx* might be intercepted before Puren could scuttle the vessel and escape liability for the hidden gold. Duverge's mistake in referring to himself as captain when speaking to the telegrapher was typical. Duverge trafficked in titles, and any time he could tout or exaggerate his own status, he would do so. His life was riddled with such dishonesty and overconfidence.[3]

In this case, it made him a fugitive. The authorities in India were certain Duverge was a criminal, as was the press. The *Cochin Chronicle* opined that since Duverge was a British subject, the French could be forced to extradite him for barratry and murder once he arrived in Europe. But no charges were ever brought against Duverge.

What happened to the crew and the gold from the *Sphynx* is unclear. A month later, the ship was recorded arriving in Cochin.[4] Presumably Puren and his crew were either captured before they could effectuate their plot, or otherwise abandoned their attempt to sink the vessel. In December, the *Sphynx* was recorded back in Mauritius for repairs, having taken on water while sailing between Karachi and Marseilles. That development likely lessened the chance that the authorities would pursue

Duverge. In 1869, the financier of the *Sphynx* filed an admiralty case in London to repossess the schooner, which was stricken from Lloyd's Register several years later.[5]

What exactly Duverge did in the year after his adventure aboard the *Sphynx* is unknown. He later told a companion that after escaping India for France, he participated in a failed conspiracy against Napoleon III. If he did so, it was no wonder the attempt failed. During this period, Napoleon III, the final monarch of France, enjoyed strong support from the public following popular economic and social reforms. In a century filled with revolutions and near revolutions in France, Baron Duverge apparently managed to join one that generated no success. Following this alleged coup attempt, Duverge related that he fled to England dressed as a priest.

In 1864, Duverge was back in Mauritius where he obtained a letter of reference from the American consul, who apparently was uninformed about the *Sphynx* matter. That August, he boarded the schooner *Ayumar*. Duverge then appeared in St. Helena, where he paid a call to the recently arrived American consul, George Gerard. At that time, St. Helena was an especially challenging assignment for an American consular officer. The British island between Brazil and Africa was small but valuable to the Confederacy as a replenishing station for ships transporting goods between Europe and the South. One of the American consul's duties was to emphasize to British officials that these blockade runners were rogue vessels that should be denied entry to port. Gerard, a naturalized citizen originally from France, would have been pleased to see a fellow French speaker appear, especially when Duverge announced he was headed to America to fight the Rebels. Following their meeting, Gerard sent a message to the War Department recommending the Mauritian for an appointment with the Union Army. Gerard regarded Durverge as a "well-intentioned young man," offered a brief history of Duverge's military experience in English, and then, slipping into his native French, related that he understood Duverge had "received a good education in Bordeaux."[6] Duverge must have been pleased when he departed St. Helena sailing northwest.

On September 14, 1864, he arrived in America. New York City would have impressed even a seasoned traveler like Duverge. While there were no skyscrapers yet, sailing into New York Harbor, Duverge would have easily spotted the spire of Trinity Church. At 281 feet, it was the tallest structure on the continent and looked down upon a city of more than a million residents, a diverse collection of inhabitants from every part of America and nearly every corner of the world. Disembarking along the docks of the Lower East Side, Duverge would have heard a cacophony of foreign tongues, as well as every conceivable accent and dialectic of the English language. It was an appropriate welcome to this country of many races, faiths, languages, and customs—a nation presently engaged in a brutal and bloody conflict with itself. That war, though fought hundreds of miles away, was never far from New York. The city's fortunes were heavily tied to the American South. Linked to textile mills upstate by canals and railroads, New York had been the distribution point for much of the cotton produced in the Southern states before the rebellion. Resistance to the war among New Yorkers was strong, exploding a year before Duverge's arrival with the Draft Riots of 1863. Impoverished white men, resentful of the draft and other effects of the war, staged violent protests throughout the island. Their animus was directed toward profiteers, draft dodgers, and freed blacks. The Draft Riots injured thousands and killed over a hundred, requiring the deployment of military forces to finally quell the violence. The army managed to limit the immediate destruction, but the underlying reasons for unrest and dissatisfaction remained when Duverge landed a year later. A few weeks after his arrival, President Lincoln only barely won New York State in the 1864 election, defeating Democrat George McClellan by fewer than seven thousand votes. Two weeks after ballots were cast, a group of eight covert Southern agents dubbed "The Confederate Army of Manhattan" entered the city. Their attempt to set fire to several New York landmarks, including P.T. Barnum's famed American Museum, failed. But their actions demonstrated that the city was hardly a bastion of stability.

Duverge had arrived at the right time for a foreigner looking to join the fight. Even in late 1864, when the war appeared to be moving strongly in the Union's favor, victory was uncertain. New troops were desperately needed, but after three years of devastating conflict, there were few remaining Americans to recruit. At the start of fighting in 1861, Washington had been optimistic that the conflict could be ended quickly using only the existing U.S. Army. That force, the so-called "regular army," was composed of professional soldiers, many of whom entered the war with significant experience from campaigns in Mexico or along the western frontier. However, their numbers were limited. At the commencement of the Civil War, the army had approximately fifteen thousand men. General Winfield Scott, the highly competent but elderly head of the army, estimated that at least another seventy thousand would be needed. After the first Battle of Manassas, the first significant engagement of the war, it was apparent that even eighty-five thousand soldiers might be insufficient. A day after the Confederacy's shocking victory at Manassas, Congress authorized the president to mobilize half a million troops.[7]

To find these men, Lincoln turned to the states. Under Article 1, Section 8 of the U.S. Constitution, each state was obligated to provide troops to the federal government "to suppress insurrection and repel invasions." The Militia Act of 1792 detailed how each state was to render support to Washington, as well as how these soldiers were to maintain readiness during times of peace. Adherence to the act by the states and their militias was erratic and rarely adequate. As such, for the duration of the conflict, Lincoln sought continued increases in manpower for the regular army. The institution of a federal draft yielded mixed results. Wealthy draftees paid for poorer men to take their places. These opportunists often deserted, escaping to again seek out opportunities as substitutes. Other conscripts elected to buy their way out of military duty by paying so-called "commutation," a phenomenon that helped, in part, spark the aforementioned 1863 Draft Riots in New York City. Immediately following the issuance of the Emancipation Proclamation in 1863, black Americans started to enlist. Eventually more than 180,000 volunteered. Because the Confederacy refused to consider black soldiers as prisoners of war, and as a matter of policy executed their white officers for inciting insurrections, Lincoln endeavored to keep black troops in positions where their chances of capture were relatively low. Accordingly, most black soldiers in the Union Army served in labor battalions and other non-combat roles.[8] It was from the state governments that the Union gained most of its fighting men. Governors recruited citizens into existing militias and sent them off to support the Northern effort. Concurrently, some regiments were organized locally and then presented to the governor for deployment. These efforts were often coordinated by a prominent local figure who then sought the governor's imprimatur to make official their status as a senior officer.

Such was the history of the 30th Massachusetts Infantry Regiment, into which Duverge enrolled as a second lieutenant in Boston on October 15, 1864. The 30th Massachusetts was established in 1861 by Benjamin Butler, a man with no legitimate military experience who used the regiment as a platform for his political aspirations. Among his first appointments was that of administrator of occupied New Orleans, to where the 30th Massachusetts was posted in 1862. While in New Orleans, Butler used the 30th Massachusetts and other units to strictly regulate the civilian population. In doing so, he gained a reputation for sternness and corruption. Butler was particularly aggressive in his conduct toward diplomatic consuls in New Orleans, whom he suspected of favoritism toward the Confederacy. Such diplomatic tension was worrisome to President Lincoln, who understood that the South's best hope of victory was to gain foreign support. Unsurprisingly, Butler was recalled from his post. He continued his political progress, however, later being elected to Congress and then the governorship of Massachusetts. The 30th Massachusetts remained in Louisiana after Butler's departure, eventually fighting its way north along the Mississippi as part of Scott's Anaconda Plan to encircle the Confederacy. The unit participated in the months-long siege of Port Hudson under General Nathaniel Banks before being redirected south to suppress remaining resistance in the now-split Confederacy. In early 1864, the regiment earned several months of leave before being repositioned to Virginia in August, where they entered the eastern theater of the Civil War.

In November 1864, Duverge joined these battle-hardened fighters in Virginia. In a letter home, First Lieutenant Henry Warren Howe recorded Duverge's arrival, where he evidently wasted no time trading on his aristocratic heritage: "I have twenty-three in my company; some of these are French and there is one Dutchman. I like the Frenchman much the best; he used to be a Sergeant Major in the French Army and is a Baron."[9]

The 30th Massachusetts was, at that time, deployed to Winchester in support of General Sheridan and his Army of the Potomac. Sheridan had been charged with neutralizing the bountiful Shenandoah Valley. It was a brutal, sanguinary task that required intense combat with the enemy and heartless destruction of civilian farms and commerce. A month before Duverge arrived in Virginia, the 30th Massachusetts, a thousand men strong at full complement, suffered 127 casualties at the Battle of Cedar Creek. Among the twelve killed were five of the regiment's eleven officers. Duverge and the other recruits from Boston were not reinforcements—they were replacements. He never saw serious combat, though. The weather had turned cold, and soon, exhausted from months of action, both armies retired to winter quarters. Occasional skirmishes did still occur, but there was little bloodshed. Three days after Duverge's arrival in Virginia, enemy cavalry attacked the 30th Regiment's position. The Rebel effort was halfhearted and resulted in no casualties on either side. There would be other minor confrontations with the Confederates that winter, but none that seriously endangered Duverge. These sporadic interactions were possibly the most heated fighting he experienced during his American service.

Duverge did not escape conflict, though. Just ten days after his arrival in Winchester, he found himself subject to a court-martial. Of the multitude of judicial processes Duverge encountered during his life, the 1864 court-martial is the one instance where he was very possibly without any serious fault. Assigned as the officer in charge of the regiment's picket, Duverge allowed a local citizen to pass through the lines with an expired note of permission. When the man reached his destination, he was granted a new, valid note from a higher-ranking officer who simultaneously dispatched a message to Lieutenant Duverge, telling him not to honor any more expired permissions. Dutifully, Duverge stopped several other citizens that day from passing through the picket without a valid note. Nevertheless, Duverge's earlier mistake was noted by his command, and he was charged with disobedience of an order. In a letter he drafted explaining his actions, Duverge cited his poor command of English and sincere attempts to adhere to the instructions, noting that the orders were ambiguous about how to handle an expired pass. He respectfully begged the court for forgiveness. Duverge penned the note in French.

The specifications of charges against Duverge were witnessed in an affidavit by two other officers: Captain J.B. Seefs, attached to the adjunct general of Massachusetts, and Major Felix Agnus, of the 165th New York Volunteers. After Duverge's senior officer submitted a letter attesting to Duverge's performance and good intentions, Major Agnus forwarded a note to the command, recommending the charges against Duverge be voided, a suggestion that was adopted.

Duverge took less than a month to land himself in trouble again. On December 14, he was arrested for "neglect to parade his guard at reveille roll call." Briefly arrested, he avoided a formal court-martial and received instead only an admonishment from the commanding officer and a letter in his service record. In January, he received permission to leave Virginia for ten days "on important personal business." What exactly he was doing or where he went is unknown, but perhaps it contributed to his puzzling promotion to first lieutenant at the end of the month. For a young officer who had entered service barely three months before, and during that period had accrued an official letter of admonishment and court-martial charges, Duverge was ascending rapidly up the ranks. It is possible he had some help. Major Felix Agnus, the same man who had sat on Duverge's court-martial panel and later recommended that the charges be voided, was his likely mentor.

Agnus was a native Frenchman whose life in many ways mirrored that of Duverge.[10] Born a year before Duverge in Lyon, Agnus spent his youth exploring Africa and the Indian Ocean before completing a journey around the world at the age of seventeen. Like Duverge, Agnus enlisted in the French Army in 1859, also fighting in Italy. Agnus and Duverge very likely shared mutual acquaintances and quite possibly knew one another during this period. Their paths temporarily diverged after Italy. Their sense of integrity also seems to have moved in different directions at this time. While Agnus's life subsequent to the French military evinced a record of honor and accomplishment, Duverge's was marked by a pattern of dishonesty and failure. In 1861, Agnus enlisted as a private in an appropriately French-inspired Zouaves regiment of New York. He saved the life of Captain Hudson Kilpatrick, the first Union officer wounded in the war, at the Battle of Big Bethel. Agnus was immediately promoted to second lieutenant. During the Peninsula Campaign the following year, he was seriously wounded, spending several months recuperating in Baltimore, where he met the daughters of local newspaper magnate Charles

Fulton. There "the wounded young Frenchmen came under their minis-trations." But personal business was swept aside when Agnus, recovered from his wounds, was promoted to captain and returned to New York to raise a regiment of black volunteers, his own regiment having been decimated since the start of hostilities. He returned to combat in 1862 in Louisiana, where Agnus was again wounded and promoted. After fighting along the Mississippi for several months, his unit was ordered west. There, during a "hand to hand fight with a Texas-horseman," Major Agnus suffered his third combat injury, a "severe saber wound." He was relocated to Virginia, where he entered service under General Sheridan. By the time Agnus encountered Duverge in late 1865, he was a veteran officer and decorated war hero.[11]

Duverge's specious court-martial charges and the accompanying let-ter in French pleading the young Mauritian's innocence likely captured Agnus's sympathies. It was a connection Duverge was to exploit again at a later date, and perhaps more than once.

In April 1865, Duverge and his regiment were relocated to just south of Washington. The wartime city seemed as much a fortress as a national capital. Encircled by a series of walls, redoubts, and artillery positions erected to protect Washington from attack, the 30th Massa-chusetts was there, in theory, to assist with the city's defense. The need for such protection at that point in the conflict was minimal, though. Since the start of April, Richmond had fallen, the Confederate govern-ment had all but evaporated, and General Lee had surrendered his Army of Northern Virginia to General Grant. Five days after the 30th Mas-sachusetts moved to the Washington area, General Johnston's Army of Tennessee, the last significant Confederate force, surrendered to General Sherman. The war was finished. The Union did suffer an exceptionally painful loss that month, though, when, on April 14, John Wilkes Booth assassinated President Lincoln. Booth evaded capture for three weeks before he was killed in Port Royal, Virginia, very near the 30th Massa-chusetts's then position. The regiment would remain there until June 1. Aside from proximity to Booth's capture, perhaps the most notable event Duverge experienced during this period was his participation in the Grand Review victory parade of May 23 and May 24. President Johnson ordered the parade with the intention of both celebrating the

The Grand Review, May 1865. Duverge's regiment was among those present in Washington, D.C. Photo by Mathew B. Brady, Library of Congress.

defeat of the Confederacy and lifting the country's spirits following Lincoln's martyrdom. More than 200,000 soldiers participated, marching down Pennsylvania Avenue in front of Mathew Brady's flashing bulbs and stands full of politicians and other dignitaries, a show of triumph following four long years of fighting. Duverge, barely six months in America, was among these men.[12]

A week after the Grand Review, Duverge relocated south to Charleston, where the war had commenced at Fort Sumter. The city had endured extraordinary hardship throughout the conflict. A two-year continuous siege marked by regular, imprecise bombardments turned the once prosperous port into ruins. The devastated city finally capitulated to the Union Army in February 1865. Yankee soldiers then entered Charleston as an occupying force, responsible for suppressing rebellion and restoring law and order. In June, Duverge's regiment was posted to "Sumter and its vicinity, remaining there for a year on provost duty."[13]

Duverge soon landed in Charleston District Jail, an institution with its own extraordinary history.

Constructed in 1802 with a significant expansion immediately before the start of the war, the city's jail was an intimidating facility. The jail occupied an acre of land and was surrounded by a twenty-foot wall. At the front of the building were two formidable fifty-foot towers topped by crenelated parapets, giving the structure a castle-like appearance. An additional two-story octagonal tower was present atop the jail during Duverge's day, making it one of Charleston's tallest occupied buildings. Constructed of reinforced concrete, the fireproof jail was built in the imposing Romanesque Revival style which is also seen in the Smithsonian Castle in Washington and many American courthouses of the era.

The jail was used to detain captured Union officers from the start of hostilities until the end of the conflict. Some of these men became pawns of the Confederates during the Siege of Charleston. Southern forces, angered by what they characterized as dishonorable, indiscriminate artillery attacks upon Charleston, relocated Union prisoners from the jail to areas of the city that were under bombardment. Federal troops then did the same with captured Confederate officers, placing them at the front of their lines and subjecting them to potential death by Southern attack. Eventually the Rebels capitulated, resulting in both sides pulling back their prisoners of war from the front. Later in his life, Duverge would claim that he was among the Union officers subject to this abuse.

He was lying, though.

Duverge's service record with the War Department provides no mention of such detention. Further, an appeal decades later from his wife for a survivor's pension makes no special claim for prisoner of war benefits. Additionally, none of Duverge's service was likely to have exposed him to capture. Most tellingly, a collection of period letters recorded by Civil War journalist David Power Conyngham suggests Duverge did not enter the jail until after hostilities had ended. Conyngham recorded an undated plea for better treatment from a "French officer" detained in the Charleston Jail. The letter was signed by "L. Duverge, Captain U.S.V."[14]

While undated, Duverge listed in that letter his rank as captain, a title he did not acquire until January 1866, almost a year after the end of the war. This fact all but confirms that Duverge was not detained in

*Charleston Jail, approximately ten years after Duverge's
stay. Library of Congress.*

the Charleston Jail as a prisoner of war, but rather that he was held as a
common prisoner months after the end of the conflict.

He was likely there because of a horse.

On June 15, 1866, during his final weeks of military service, Duverge
executed a document in his role as a provost officer. In that capacity,
he was one of hundreds of Union officers responsible for administering
martial law in South Carolina. The document Duverge drafted granted
a Mr. Brock possession and ownership of a mare. The title recorded a
payment of $63.45 and noted that "anyone cannot make any complaint
or claims" for the horse. In actuality, someone could make a claim for
the horse: its rightful owner. Later records show that shortly after Brock
purchased the horse from Duverge, Brock was approached by a man
who produced "undoubtable evidence" that showed the animal to be his

property. The rightful owner explained that several men from Duverge's company had borrowed the horse, but Duverge had then converted the property to his own while readying to demuster from the army in July 1866. It was probably at this time, as Duverge was preparing to return to Boston, that he was detained in the Charleston Jail. His stay there, however, was brief; less than a month later, he was in Boston. It is very likely that Duverge slipped away from the jail because of assistance from Felix Agnus, the same French-speaking officer who had aided him in evading punishment for his court-martial in Virginia the year before. In 1866, Agnus was serving as the inspector general of the South Carolina Department, a capacity which would have allowed him to influence the case to Duverge's benefit. Regardless of how Duverge escaped from Charleston, Brock was undaunted and, two months later, filed a civilian complaint in the state capital, charging Duverge with fraud. A week following the initiation of that action, the South Carolina military provost forwarded the complaint to Hart's Island in New York City (now called "Hart Island"). Hart's Island was a federal facility used to house Confederate prisoners of war, as well as court-martial detainees. The base served as a clearing house for soldiers returning to civilian life in the northeast. Officials attempted to sort out the matter by contacting Duverge.

The response received was typical for Duverge.

On August 22, 1866, a letter was sent from Boston to Hart's Island, allegedly from "L. Rusnett." The writer claimed to represent "Baron Duverge," who was "quite unwell with chills and fever, a disease he contracted while in the service." The author offered Duverge's muddled, unconvincing response. Duverge claimed the horse had been rightfully acquired on behalf of the federal government (ignoring claims from the original owner that Duverge's men had stolen it). Duverge further claimed that it was necessary for him to sell the horse to pay off "little debts" he had incurred in his capacity as an officer. Duverge additionally alleged that, when sold, the horse was actually lame. Since the animal had no value, he argued, he had not misappropriated any government resources. Instead, Duverge submitted, he had actually enriched the U.S. Treasury by using the proceeds from a worthless asset to pay off debts he had accrued on behalf of the government. Somewhat contradictory to the claim that the horse was lame, Duverge's response also offered that the property was sold at fair value and that Brock had not been defrauded. The letter concludes by asserting that the charges brought against Duverge were from another officer acting "maliciously and revengefully."

The handwriting in this letter is unmistakably Duverge's.

A plea of innocence wrapped in obfuscation, Hart's Island had received a standard Duverge response to charges. In a fashion he displayed throughout his lifetime, Duverge would commit some sort of illegality, ranging from petty theft to homicide, and then defend himself by citing every conceivable excuse and mitigating factor. Complaints of ill health. An inability to understand English. Mention of his brief service with the American military. Citations to his aristocratic heritage. All that was missing from Duverge's Hart's Island reply was an appeal to faith, which was another of his regular ploys.

Duverge's earlier letter from Charleston Jail showed a similar arrogance and perhaps hypocrisy. Conyngham records how Duverge, "being placed with some negroes, after arrest, felt very indignant and became very excited." Duverge, it seemed, a Union officer in a city that had been liberated in part due to the brave and honorable service of black Northern troops, objected to being held among others because of their race. Such views were of course not uncommon during this era, even among those who fought against slavery. It was one thing to free the slaves; another to be living among them. Advocates for complete racial equality were a small minority in post-war America. Political attempts to improve the station of black Americans encountered significant obstacles. President Johnson vetoed the Civil Rights Act of 1866 and opposed the ratification of the Fourteenth Amendment, which granted citizenship to freed persons. Duverge's letter, almost certainly written in mid-1866, clearly demonstrates that he harbored a degree of racial animus typical for the time.

Of course, he was something of an outsider among American whites. A Catholic from an obscure island in the Indian Ocean, Duverge spoke heavily accented English and knew little about American customs. It is possible that he was not entirely of European extraction. Although Duverge emphasized his paternal French ancestry, his mother's line might have included ancestors of mixed race. In different official reports, he was characterized at varying times as "light-skinned," "dark," and "very dark." What was certain was that Duverge was every bit an elitist, or at least an aspiring one. He frequently mentioned his "baron" title and European education in attempts to impress or intimidate others. Duverge regularly displayed dismissiveness and even cruelty toward subordinates and those he deemed less important than himself. And as a prisoner, as his later life would amply demonstrate, Duverge held a sense of entitlement and arrogance that made him an especially difficult detainee. While he knew how to use influence and charm, when that failed, he defaulted to conde- scension and disagreeableness. Duverge was an inherently selfish person. Yet somehow, despite his record as a court-martialed horse thief with no serious American combat experience and only a limited command of English, he later earned himself a presidential appointment.

Duverge had been seeking such a position since even before he arrived in America. His initial efforts were directed at securing a position in the Union Army. He settled for the 30th Massachusetts only after Duverge failed to receive a commission in the regular army. Once commissioned in Massachusetts, Duverge continued to try and join the U.S. Army. Beginning in January 1865, he commenced a lobbying effort among his superiors to earn him transfer to the federal service. Many approached the War Department with support for Duverge's capacities and wor- thiness as an officer. But while Duverge impressed some in his chain of command, it is notable that his direct commanding officer, Colonel William Dudley, qualified his support for the young lieutenant. Duverge would be ready for ascension to the regular army, Dudley noted, "when he becomes fully acquainted and familiar with our language and service." As such, the appeals from his advocates in Massachusetts failed to secure him the regular army commission he so desired.

After the war, Duverge sought to forgo protocol and find his own way to success, as was his habit. In September 1866 (likely after he resolved the complaint regarding the horse in South Carolina), Duverge bypassed proper channels and penned a letter directly to President John- son. That communique showed either tremendous progress in his com- mand of English or the assistance of a capable English-speaking editor. Duverge broadened his request from previous petitions, asking President Johnson for an appointment to any "employment with the government,"

Duverge's American calling card, in French.

mentioning that he was multilingual and now a resident of Boston. He included several recommendations as well as his calling card. That card advertised Duverge as an American officer but also noted he was a baron. It was written in French.

It is doubtful Duverge's appeal ever reached President Johnson, the entire packet being referred back to the War Department the day after it was received at the Executive Mansion. Buried in Duverge's attempt to persuade the president was a copy of a letter he had previously submitted to the secretary of war. That letter gives hints of Duverge's past and future in Madagascar. Duverge wrote that while serving in the French Navy he had saved a man from drowning and had "also received, at the crowning of Radama II of Madagascar, the 'cross of honour.'" Presumably the man he saved from drowning was in Malagasy waters.

The crowning of Radama II took place in September 1862. If Duverge did visit Antananarivo for the ceremony, he did not do so in an official capacity. A British delegation sent from Mauritius to applaud the new king remained in the capital until October 21. The British representatives noted that a delegation "from the French was to be expected in Madagascar . . . but no such accredited mission had arrived." What was French and present in Antananarivo that September, according to British writers, was a handful of "French adventurers." The other possibility is that Duverge visited Madagascar the following July, when Radama II received both a French and yet another British delegation, formally recognizing his coronation.[15] However, this would have left Duverge little time to carry out his attempted swindle of the *Sphynx* off of Colombo just a few weeks later, making it far more likely that Duverge was in

Madagascar in 1862, likely one of the "adventurers" noted by the British representatives. Regardless of when he was there, Duverge's presence at the Court of Radama, the son of Queen Ranavalona I, is significant given his future endeavors in Madagascar. Duverge would have been in Antananarivo as Joseph Lambert, previously banished from the island for his failed coup attempt, returned to the island to enforce his famous charter. Inevitably the two French-speakers would have met and exchanged views of the mysterious but promising land. It seems likely that this early exposure to the potential windfalls of escapades in Madagascar is what piqued Duverge's later interests in the island.

In 1866, though, Duverge's focus was on finding a livelihood in the United States. On October 4, he became an American citizen in Boston, barely two years after his arrival in the country. Then, as now, naturalization required abandonment of other citizenship. As Duverge's place of birth was Mauritius, his renouncement of previous citizenship saw him abjuring "all allegiance . . . to every foreign prince, potentate, state or sovereignty . . . particularly Victoria, Queen of the United Kingdom," despite him being far more tied to France than Great Britain. American citizenship vested Duverge, for a period, with a somewhat stable life. He spent the next decade and a half as a mariner, showing up in manifests and port records from France to Georgia, from Oregon to Cuba.

However, he was not always a model sailor.

In September 1873, Duverge was the first mate aboard the *Albertina*, a Boston-based bark engaged in trade with West Africa. Two incidents during Duverge's tenure with the *Albertina* display his tendency toward excessive discipline and opportunism. In the first, he was left in charge of the vessel while the captain ventured ashore for a few days. During this period, Duverge had the ship's cook locked in the topgallant forecastle for a day for drunkenness. This was no small punishment. The *Albertina* was afloat in the tropics in September. Conditions below deck would have been dank and rancid. Detaining the crew member there, well after he was sober, was exceptionally strict. Duverge had already been strongly critical of the cook's work and disposition before this incident; it would appear that the captain's absence gave Duverge the authority he needed to act. Duverge recorded the punishment in the ship's log and had the crew affix their signatures, attesting that his statement about the cook's drunkenness and properness of the punishment was correct. The ship's cook refused to sign, however, and upon the captain's return, he was put ashore for his behavior, despite his protests that his transgressions had been minimal and that Duverge was simply power hungry.

The captain should have listened.

Soon after, four of the eight crew members who had signed Duverge's statement in the ship's log deserted. Then, if the captain was not already certain Duverge was a less-than-ideal first mate, Duverge feigned illness. A seemingly healthy man of thirty when he boarded the *Albertina* in Boston a few months before (he lied about his age; Duverge was actually thirty-three), Duverge suddenly described himself as "dying" and in desperate need of a physician. He insisted that he must go ashore immediately for medical treatment. The skeptical captain deposited Duverge in Accra and then waited onboard for him to recover so the *Albertina* could proceed with its voyage. Two weeks later, Duverge transmitted hundreds of dollars of medical bills and associated invoices to the *Albertina* for payment (including a receipt for a bottle of champagne). The captain's suspicions increased. Upon investigation, he learned that the first mate's illness had been brief, if ever existent. Sources onshore advised that Duverge had in actuality spent most of his two weeks not as an invalid, but seeking an appointment with the British governor in Cape Coast.

The details of that effort were elucidated a decade later, where Duverge claimed in a letter to have participated in the "Ashantee War" under the command of "Colonel Festings." The Ashantee War was the Third Anglo-Ashanti War of 1873, which did indeed occur while Duverge was ashore in Accra. The war was part of a series of conflicts between the British and Ashanti tribes of the interior. For decades, London had maintained a nebulous protectorate over the coast, balancing relations with local tribes and the regionally powerful Ashanti. Periodically, interests would clash. The 1873 war, in fact, ran for two years and was precipitated by an Ashanti attempt to invade British-held territory. The "Colonel Festings," under whom Duverge claimed to have served, was his misremembering of Colonel Francis Festing, the commander of a two hundred-strong contingent of British Marines who arrived from England to push back the Ashanti. Although British holdings were under constant threat of Ashanti attack during Duverge's two weeks on land, his claim of participation in the war is dubious. There are no records of him serving with Festing, and among the numerous times Duverge boasted about military service, he only once mentioned "the Ashantee War." What is most likely is he tried to join the war but was rejected. Festing's men were British regulars. That is not to say London used only its own forces to prosecute the war; African auxiliaries were an important part of Festing's campaign. But he would have been unlikely to take on a strange Mauritian who claimed both British and American citizenship while speaking with a French accent, especially after a ship captain appeared and accused Duverge of desertion.

Once confronted by the *Albertina*'s captain, Duverge had no choice but to return to the vessel, lest he face desertion charges. The bark then started its voyage back to Boston. There, the ship owners, citing Duverge's invented illness, attendant bills, and dereliction of duty, paid him $100 and sent him on his way. Duverge immediately sued in admiralty court, claiming he was due an additional $300. He was correct in the sense that the original contract he had signed with the owners promised him $400 in exchange for his service. But while the owners had ample reason to argue Duverge had breached those terms during his champagne-sipping, job-hunting sojourn in Accra, an 1874 decision by Judge John Lowell awarded Duverge the balance of his contract. That holding was reached principally because there was an absence of evidence about Duverge's conduct while on land. The judge held that because Duverge had appeared sick while onboard, it was reasonable to presume that illness had continued once ashore as well, notwithstanding the substantial evidence that suggested Duverge was malingering.

Achieving yet another legal success when he was clearly the wrong party likely emboldened Duverge, especially since this evasion of responsibility had been at sea, an area where accountability was no small matter. Shirking one's duties aboard a vessel was serious business in the nineteenth century. Shipmasters, be they the captain or the first mate in the absence of the captain, were charged with administering all aspects of a vessel's life. A competent officer was not just a skilled navigator, they were strong leaders who understood how to nurture and maintain control over a crew. A capable officer could gain the respect of his men while maintaining an appropriate distance. Duverge lacked these skills.

Throughout his time at sea, Duverge too often relied upon discipline and often excessively harsh discipline.

Confident with his success in the *Albertina* matter, Duverge gained an American captain's license the following year. He then applied for an American passport. Duverge's application notes that he was 5'10" in height with blue eyes, dark brown hair, and a dark complexion. For the next several years, he commanded vessels between France and the United States, settling into a comfortable life and taking up residence in New York. Duverge rented a home near Washington Square. The structure is long since gone, but Henry James's 1881 novel *Washington Square* offers a sense of homes from the era: "red brick, with granite copings and an enormous fanlight over the door, standing in a street within five minutes walk of city hall." Duverge's career ascending, he seemed positioned as a man of success.

On November 22, 1878, he married Emily Simmons, the daughter of a moderately successful merchant from Norfolk, Virginia. She was sixteen years younger than Duverge. The ceremony was conducted by Reverend Thomas Gallaudet Jr. Thomas's father, Thomas Gallaudet Sr., was the co-founder of Gallaudet University, America's first institution of higher learning for the hearing impaired. Like his father, Rev-

The only known photo of Louis Duverge, likely taken in Boston soon after the war.

erend Gallaudet had committed his life to helping the deaf. In 1852, he established a church for the deaf, St. Ann's Episcopalian, in Washington Square. Several years later, the junior Gallaudet opened a St. Ann's-affiliated boardinghouse for the deaf in Poughkeepsie. While St. Ann's offered mass for non-deaf parishioners at the time of Duverge's marriage, most of its services were conducted in sign language, and nearly all of its congregants were, as the condition was then termed, "deaf-mute."

Duverge's residence was only a short walk from St. Ann's. Perhaps this is why he selected Reverend Gallaudet to administer his marriage. Equally likely, Duverge enjoyed the association with the honorable reverend, who was well-known as a theologian and advocate for the less fortunate. Gallaudet's familiarity with Duverge was likely not as thorough, though. Throughout his life, Duverge identified as Catholic, a faith Gallaudet would have been unwilling to marry into his church. As was Duverge's custom, he almost certainly lied, telling Gallaudet that he was Episcopalian or some other palatable Protestant denomination. Such was the way Duverge entered married life.

CHAPTER THREE

Duverge the Adventurer

Marriage did not force Duverge to put down roots, though he did secure a position that kept him in the United States, at least temporarily. In 1880, Duverge received charge of the *Nokomis*, Maryland industrialist E. M. Paddleford's yacht. Duverge captained the luxurious vessel between Long Island and Nantucket in the summertime, and cruised the Carolinas and Georgia during cooler months. While this was certainly an improvement over previous work, Duverge still hoped for a federal appointment.

So did others, among them Charles J. Guiteau. Guiteau was a failed attorney with narcissistic tendencies who spent the 1880 presidential campaign season giving a series of sparsely attended speeches in support of Republican nominee James Garfield. Guiteau's efforts were entirely unsolicited and in no way contributed to Garfield's victory in November. But in the weeks following the new president's inauguration, Guiteau confronted officials, demanding a consular assignment as compensation for his campaigning. Making no progress with these requests, in July 1881, Guiteau followed Garfield to the Baltimore and Potomac Railroad Station, where he then shot the president with a revolver. Garfield died two months later, on September 22, 1881. Vice President Chester A. Arthur immediately ascended to the presidency. The change in executives led to speculation about the new cabinet, as well as opportunities for lesser office seekers. Guiteau, the aspiring consul now headed to the gallows, had unwittingly unleashed a new group of job seekers upon the capital. Attempting to avoid those petitioners and conspiratorial inquiries that insinuated Arthur himself might have suborned Guiteau's attack, the new president sequestered himself in the White House for four weeks. It was not until the celebration of the centennial of the Battle of Yorktown, on October 19, 1881, that he finally appeared in public. There, Arthur gave a speech commemorating the Yorktown victory before a crowd of thousands, including Felix Agnus.

Agnus was the Union officer who had likely helped Duverge avoid a court-martial in Virginia and prolonged imprisonment in Charleston. After ending his military service as a brevet general, Agnus settled in Baltimore, where he married well and entered publishing. Eventually he gained control of the *Baltimore American*, then the city's largest paper. Duverge probably secured his command of the *Nokomis* through Agnus, a close friend of Paddleford and other prominent Marylanders. But Agnus's biggest gift to Duverge originated at the Yorktown centennial, where Agnus recommended the young Mauritian-American to the head of the French delegation, General Georges Boulanger. Boulanger's support would be pivotal to Duverge's search for an appointment. While Agnus was a person of some influence in the United States, Boulanger was a man of significant importance throughout Europe. He had first come to prominence for bravery while fighting on behalf of Napoleon III (the same monarch whom Duverge claimed he had attempted to stage a coup d'etat to depose in 1864). Boulanger soldiered from Italy to Indochina to Saarbrücken, gaining a reputation as a capable, fearless soldier. Following the Franco-Prussian War and the establishment of the Third French Republic, he helped suppress a group of radical progressives who briefly took control of Paris. For his loyalty to the republican government, Boulanger was promoted to general. His improvements to military regulations enhanced efficiency and earned him popularity throughout the ranks. By the time Boulanger arrived in America in 1881 to celebrate French assistance rendered during America's War for Independence, he was one of his country's most popular public figures and a major force in French foreign policy. In later years, Boulanger would promote *revanchism*, his somewhat murky nationalistic political ideology that called for revenge against Germany and a restoration of France's proper place among the global powers. His coalition of disaffected working-class citizens and nostalgic royalists saw him as a panacea to France's economic and political troubles. Boulanger's popularity grew as the public increasingly viewed him as an alternative to the existing power structure in France. For a time in the 1880s, Boulanger was widely considered a future leader of France, either elected or otherwise.

The French delegation that arrived in New York in 1881 was unencumbered by such serious political considerations. Boulanger's journey to America was symbolic. The jaunt across the Atlantic was expected to be heavy on pomp and light on drama. He was to lead a group of military and civil dignitaries on a tour of the eastern United States to showcase France's contributions to the American Experiment before participating in the formal Yorktown centennial ceremony. Boulanger's visit was not entirely devoid of excitement, though. While asleep in a hotel room in Philadelphia, Boulanger woke to encounter a burglar. The general sprang from his bed, grabbed his sword, and immediately disarmed the criminal.[1] That, no doubt, provided a good story when Boulanger encountered Agnus a week later in Yorktown.

The two likely already knew each. It is also possible that Boulanger knew Duverge. All three men had served in the French Army in Italy, though in different units. Even if Boulanger had never met Duverge, he likely would sympathize with a fellow Frenchman who had fought for the Union cause. Boulanger's own brother had been killed while fighting as a Union volunteer. Regardless of whether Boulanger did or did not have any previous association with Duverge, at some point his name emerged during a conversation with Agnus. Boulanger agreed with Agnus that the French-speaking Mauritian might be better used as an American political appointee than steering yachts around Martha's Vineyard for pleasure cruisers. Were Duverge nominated to some position of influence in the federal government, his eventual service there might benefit American and French interests. Accordingly, Agnus and Boulanger proposed to the State Department that Duverge be made American consul to Mauritius.[2] Someone paid attention to their recommendation. On February 8, 1882, the *Washington Evening Star* reported: "A Baltimore delegation was at the White House today in the interest of Commander Du Verge, of Baltimore, for a consular position in the Indian Ocean. The delegation consisted of General W. W. Ross, General Felix Agnus of *The Baltimore American*, and Captain Richardson. All the members of the delegation and the gentleman they were on hand to advance were soldiers in the Union Army and all were badly wounded."[3]

For two decades, Duverge had cultivated the image of an accomplished gentleman while simultaneously suppressing his history of criminality, oscillating between prison and promotion. Now a cadre of esteemed officers was advocating for him in person at the White House, with the weight of France's greatest military man behind the request. A few weeks later, the success of the White House meeting was confirmed. On March 7, 1882, Louis Leopold Du Rothier Duverge was finally granted a position in the federal government: a Department of State consular appointment. Duverge's history of mutiny, courts-martial, fraud, and malingering were buried in the past. Unfortunately for Duverge, his new position was not in the Indian Ocean. Instead of Mauritius or some other Indian Ocean port, Duverge was to assume charge of the consular post in St. Paul de Loanda, Portuguese West Africa (present-day Luanda, Angola; referred to, even during Duverge's time, as simply "Angola"). For Duverge, Angola's location on the wrong side of Africa was not the only disappointment. Loanda was a low-paying assignment.

While there, it was understood that Duverge could pursue other income opportunities. Such allowances made some degree of self-dealing a near certainty but were essential during a time when support from Washington was minimal, particularly in southern Africa. Consular staff in the region might go years without ever seeing another American official. Communications consisted of the diplomatic pouch or telegraph, both of which were facilitated (and subject to espionage by) foreign powers. Tangible support from Washington was minimal. The State Department was habitually truant in supplying flagstaffs, stationery, postage, and other staples of nineteenth-century diplomacy to facilities overseas. And there were never-ending disputes about expense accounts and distribution of salaries—for those officers who received salaries.

Per an 1856 law, the consular service was divided into three classes of employees.[4] Those of the first class, typically consul generals who administered a mission in a sovereign state, received annual salaries between $1,500 and $7,500 per year (approximately $50,000 and $250,000 in 2025, respectively). These professional officers were prohibited from engaging in any private business. For example, Consul General John Francis in Lisbon, technically Duverge's direct supervisor since Angola was a Portuguese colony, earned $5,000 per year. Employees of the second class received between $500 and $1,000. These officers were permitted to work outside their consular duties, provided there was no conflict of interest in those efforts. Duverge belonged to this group, receiving $1,000 per year in salary from the State Department (approximately $35,000 in 2025). Most officers of this rank were consular agents like Duverge or vice-consuls at larger posts, such as London or Mexico City. The third class of consular employees consisted of vice-consuls at smaller posts, like Loanda. These men, and they were all men in the nineteenth century, were unpaid but could derive income from the processing fees they collected while providing basic consular services, such as receiving mail or notarizing bills of lading. Duverge's vice-consul in Angola, Robert Newton, was just such a case. A U.S. citizen, Newton was appointed State Department vice-consul in Loanda in 1868. Throughout his tenure, he worked concurrently for the State Department while simultaneously serving as a British vice-consul. Newton also ran one of the largest trading houses in Loanda.

It was into this entrepreneurial world of diplomacy that Duverge entered when he and his wife arrived in Loanda in June 1882.

For the first two and a half centuries of Portuguese rule, slavery was the primary industry of Angola. In 1836, however, Lisbon joined the other European states and prohibited the trade of slaves across the Atlantic, though maintaining the practice in its colonies. In 1869, following pressure from the British and American governments, slavery was prohibited inside Angola as well. The slave trade in Angola persisted, however, a clandestine reality that remained very much alive at the time of Duverge's arrival.

Angola, then as now, was a place of great, undeveloped opportunities. Despite the country's rich interior, an area blessed with mineral wealth and extraordinary agricultural potential, Angola still lacked an economic replacement for the trade of human beings. Loanda's harbor was superb, but the country produced few goods to export. The colonial capital was dusty, with poor sanitation and few luxuries, though improvements were slowly being implemented. Public buildings were under construction, the city's roads near the port were decent, and there was talk of a railroad. Mary Kingsley, the renowned British travel writer, visited the city in August 1893, shortly after Angola's first railroad commenced operations.

She characterized Loanda as "the only beautiful city" on the entire west coast of Africa.[5]

Duverge's early reports to Washington provided his assessment of the town, as well as the region's suitability for investment. He offered suggestions for how America might improve its reputation in the region. As United States diplomats in far-flung ports still do today, Duverge recommended that a visit from a U.S. naval vessel would enhance America's standing. Specifically, he judged that "a man of war is needed at least twice a year on this coast."[6] His later reports expanded on his initial impressions, detailing the volume of imports into the colony and what items remained in demand. He shared the nature and prices of locally produced goods, giving estimates of ivory and agricultural exports. Duverge offered information about gold and other mining opportunities in Angola. He gave opinions on infrastructure, transportation, and customs obligations. And he detailed the volume and nature of the illicit slave trade in Angola. These early messages remain of value to scholars today.[7] Throughout his reports, Duverge's prose was precise but not uninteresting:

> The temperature is agreeable, the thermometer seldom rising above 23 degrees in the shade. The summer or rainy season is more properly divided into two seasons, the "small rain and the big rain." On the 18th of October, when we have seen the sun in our zenith, small showers begin to fall in the afternoon until the 22d day of December, when the sun attains its greatest southern declination; from that date until the 24th of February, when we again have the sun at our zenith, the weather remains changeable, while in March and April the rains come down in torrents of sometimes twelve and sixteen hours' duration, inundating the country and swelling the rivers.[8]

His English skills far-improved from his Civil War letters, Duverge displays here the sort of objective yet engaging writing that remains essential in diplomatic correspondence. State Department officials in Washington, during Duverge's era and today, lack the time to read in detail every message sent from every embassy and every consulate. Capable diplomats learn early to craft communiques that are both factual and vivid. Disenchantment soon crept into Duverge's messages, though. His opinion of Loanda's climate reversed, and he increasingly complained of health issues. He started to take frequent leave outside of the city, characterizing the capital as unlivable. In October 1882, Duverge asked for "standing permission" to escape Loanda because of chronic sickness, claiming a need to go either "north or south" within Angola. Once permission was granted, he did just that. He visited Benguela, a smaller, breezier, quieter port to the south, less prone to the outbreaks of "green fever" and smallpox that plagued Loanda. He found respite along the Kwanza River, later relating to the State Department that British and other foreign merchants there were pursuing trade opportunities while American traders were absent. He wrote frequently of Angola's inhospitable environment, enclosing in one of his despatches an insect floating in alcohol. According to Duverge, it was a sample of "one of the jiggers, which is [sic] the scourge of Angola." Duverge sent news of a macabre hospital fire in Cabinda in the country's north ("it is reported that several of the smallpox sufferers were left in their houses and burnt to a crisp").

In another despatch, he complained about how he, unlike the consular agents from other nations, lacked a dedicated boat for his own use. Washington's reaction to this message was one of befuddlement. When asked to explain why he thought the government should fund such extravagance, Duverge wrapped himself in the flag in his response: "If I permitted myself to make such request it is because every consul, vice consul, and consular agent here, have a boat from their government, and I, a consul representing so great a nation as the United States, cannot be less in representing my country than the poorest consular agent of Loanda."[9]

He did not get a boat.

As surprisingly fluent as Duverge was in his communications and as detailed as his writings were about Angola, he was an administratively incompetent appointee. In November 1882, Duverge was compelled to write a contrite letter to Washington, timidly acknowledging "the incorrect numbering of my despatches, for which I feel very sorry."[10] His misnumbering habit continued, however. In December, Duverge engaged three new vice-consuls in other Angolan cities without permission from Washington. He was admonished but retained his position. The State Department reprimanded Duverge twice. The first was for a failure to submit quarterly accounts on time, a seminal duty of any consular agent. In a separate incident, his Washington chain of command was puzzled by a letter he had mistakenly sent to the State Department instead of to its intended recipients. That communication pleaded for "owners, agents and masters of American whaling vessels and others" to consider Angola as a stopping point between America and other destinations in Africa. Duverge's letter presented a far different impression of Loanda from the dreary, unclean, disease-infested city he recently described to his superiors. The mis-posted message lauded Loanda's new hotels with their "refreshing meals," inexpensive port fees, and affordable provisions. He touted the availability of hospitals, ship repairs, and regular communications via steamers to England and Portugal.[11] Durverge's letter was not a recitation of facts designed to give American businessmen information they could use to determine if they should or should not invest in Angola, a task among his primary duties. Instead, it was an attempt to induce American maritime concerns to replace Monrovia or Cape Town with Loanda as a port of call in the African trade. Such a change may or may not have benefited American commerce, but it would certainly have aided consular agent Duverge. The more frequently American vessels stopped in Loanda, the more frequently he could pocket consular service fees. One of his superiors in Washington scratched a note upon Duverge's advertisement letter: "this seems not to have been intended for the Department." Another unknown Washington reader agreed, adding "Yes!". No formal consequences followed.

In some sense, Duverge had little to worry about regarding his performance in Angola. Turnover was frequent in consular positions, especially among the consulates in southern Africa. For example, Duverge's predecessor in Loanda was William Hannibal Thomas, at least on paper. Thomas, a black Civil War combat veteran who realized a degree of fame writing self-denigrating books about the potential of former slaves, was appointed to Loanda by President Hayes in 1878. He never reached Angola; instead, he spent months traipsing around America, boasting about his title as a soon-to-be consular officer. During a spree of passing bad checks in the name of the federal government, Thomas appeared before a reverend in Massachusetts, seeking a loan. The reverend advised the State Department that a "colored man with one arm" (Thomas's arm had been shot off in combat near Fort Fisher, North Carolina, in 1865) was claiming to be a consular officer who had served two years in Angola. The writer found this impossible: "If he has lived in Loanda two years it is longer than anyone else has lived there. The consuls generally die in 4 months!" The agent who succeeded Duverge, Robert Davis, had an experience with Loanda similar to Thomas. After procrastinating for six months, Davis finally boarded a steamer to Liverpool with onward passage to Angola. Once in England, though, Davis determined he was too ill to continue and instead resigned his consular position and returned to America, never making it to Africa. This pattern was common for posts like Loanda. As such, the State Department had a high degree of tolerance for Duverge's inactivity, provided he was at least in Africa. It was expected that he would not last long in Angola, an expectation that Vice-Consul Newton, who desired to run the consulate alone, certainly held as well.

In addition to reporting on commercial opportunities in Angola, Duverge was charged with assisting Americans in distress. The majority of these cases involved mariners stranded onshore, usually after a shipwreck or desertion. As American trading vessels rarely visited Angola, most of these incidents involved whaling ships. One of the few instances where Duverge interceded to help Americans who were not sailors was in the Silveira brothers' case. Of Portuguese ancestry but both American citizens, the men were arrested in Angola in 1883 on counterfeiting charges. Around the same time, the Parliament in Lisbon authorized banishment to the colonies for Portuguese convicted of certain offenses. Colonial authorities jailed the two men indefinitely as they tried to unravel what to do with offenders who had committed an offense suitable for banishment while already in the destination for banishment. The case became further complicated once it was established that the Silveiras held American citizenship. Upon learning of their incarceration, Duverge dutifully reported the matter to Washington. In doing so, he invoked some of the same prejudice he had evinced from the Charleston Jail cell years before, writing about the incarceration of the Silveira brothers, "I am ashamed to admit that they are American citizens and that they are lock and key with negroes and robbers of all grades."[12] The State Department agreed that the Silveiras merited assistance, and instructed Duverge's nominal superior in Lisbon, Consul General John Francis, to meet with Portugal's foreign minister on the question. Francis's presentation was persuasive; soon after the request from the United States, King Luís I of Portugal granted clemency to the two prisoners. Francis wrote to Duverge in July 1883, imploring him to hold the authorities in Loanda accountable and to see that the brothers were released and returned to America immediately. Duverge, apparently having lost interest in the case, did nothing that summer.

He was likely too busy outside of Loanda. Ostensibly, this was so he could escape unhealthy Loanda and report important information back to Washington; to some extent, he did. Duverge's study of slavery in Angola offered that the "negro or slave traffic in this province still continues, in full force." He wrote to the State Department, "I have been following a real slave business," noting that "thousands have been shipped to St. Thomas [present day Sao Tome, which was then a major coffee and cacao producer] and not one has returned." Duverge shared that he knew of a man in Loanda who had purchased two slaves from a trader, executing a "contract" for five years of work from the two, though in reality, the document was only a legal gesture: both were enslaved. The situation was even more egregious in the provinces. Duverge reported that "throughout the interior the purchase or barter is affected as of old, without even the semblance of a contract being made." His most astounding communication to Washington involved his wife. Duverge wrote that she was returning to America with a singular companion: "a live specimen of slave traffic in Africa, a stolen child given to her by a respectable white merchant for the simple reason that she was too young to be sold."[13] In addition to his examination of slavery, Duverge investigated political intrigue along Angola's northern border. The nascent Scramble for Africa affected all of the region, but no place more than Congo. Visiting Portuguese holdings in the area, Duverge reported that the "strong impression here is that a great disturbance is expected in the upper congo very soon." His sense of impending trouble in Congo would prove to be true in the most personal sense.

After barely a year in Angola, Duverge was finished with the place. He was ready to leave his long sought-after consul position, but not without first attempting to find a better post. Duverge abruptly informed

Washington that Angola was unworthy of an American presence. He reported that trade opportunities for the United States were minimal, despite some initial impressions suggesting otherwise, and that there was no reason to maintain a consular presence in Loanda. When that failed to yield reassignment, Duverge adjusted his messaging, focusing on his health. He argued that he was too sick to remain in Angola. In June, Duverge wrote that he was uncertain how he might continue: ailing, alone, idle, and boatless. He begged for another assignment, no doubt hoping something in the Indian Ocean might emerge.

Receiving no such news, in July, Duverge informed Vice-Consul Newton that he was going to Banana, the port city at the mouth of the Congo River. Duverge claimed this journey was a consular necessity. American interests in the region needed to be investigated. Duverge estimated he would be away from post for a lengthy amount of time, particularly since after concluding his work in Banana, he would then go to Europe on personal leave to recover his health. Clearly, he would be unable to attend to matters in Loanda while away, so he and Newton struck a private agreement whereby Newton would collect $10 per month of Duverge's consular agent salary in exchange for keeping the consulate running on his own. Duverge asked that letters be sent to a French trading house in Banana, not the Portuguese or British houses that would have been more typical for an American consul. He then departed Loanda on apparent good terms with Newtown.

In actuality, the two were simultaneously scheming against one another.

Before Duverge left for Banana, he wrote to Washington that Newton was corrupt and disloyal. His goal is unknown. Maybe he had a personal or professional dislike of Newton. Or perhaps, as was so often the case with Duverge, he simply enjoyed exerting authority. Newton, meanwhile, also wrote to the State Department, claiming that he was forced to resign because Duverge had left him alone and unsupported in Loanda. Further, Duverge had taken with him to Banana essential consular files, including the papers and seals necessary to send proper despatches to Washington. Duverge had even taken the key to the safe.

Newton was bluffing about resigning. He hoped that by threatening to quit, he could convince the State Department to appoint him as acting consular agent, a role he had encumbered multiple times since his initial appointment in 1868 and a position with ample opportunities for side business. In communications to Washington, Newtown slyly included a rumor that Duverge was not in Banana conducting State Department business, but job prospecting.

Duverge's arrival in Banana places him there during the early years of King Leopold II of Belgium's involvement in the region. Leopold's role in the opening of central Africa remains one of the most debated but no doubt troubling cases in the continent's history. The Belgian king had first indicated an interest in Congo in 1876 when he invited scholars and diplomats to Brussels to attend what he characterized as a geographic conference, wherein the future of central Africa would be discussed. Casting himself as more concerned with altruistic pursuits than exploitation, Leopold created a series of seemingly apolitical associations to study and eventually administer the Congo region over the next several years.[14] At the time, his work was widely regarded as selfless and progressive.

In 1878, Leopold, who had never visited Africa himself, recruited famed journalist and explorer Henry Morton Stanley to run his new association.

Stanley had risen to prominence seven years earlier on the other side of the continent when he located the missing Dr. David Livingstone along the shores of Lake Tanganyika. Whether Stanley had actually uttered "Dr. Livingstone, I presume?" at that moment is undetermined. What is indisputable is that when the news of that meeting reached the outside world, Stanley became an international celebrity. Eschewing fame, Stanley returned to Africa in 1874 and led a nearly three-year-long expedition from Zanzibar to the Atlantic Ocean, making him the first European to transit the region. Stanley's accomplishments were not without criticism, though. He was attacked for being unnecessarily violent toward Africans, an unjust claim relative to the conduct of many contemporary European explorers, let alone the barbarity of the Arab traders who were then vigorously depopulating certain parts of the continent. One reason Stanley received unmerited criticism was that he was considered an American. In truth, he was born into a fractured home in Wales, where he grew up in extreme poverty. His name at birth was actually John Rowlands.

Rowlands escaped to New Orleans, adopting his new name and identity. During the Civil War, he fought for the Confederacy before being captured at Shiloh. To avoid the high risk of death in a Yankee prison camp, Stanley enlisted in the Union Army and later the navy. He then sought his fortune along the American frontier, discovering an aptitude for journalism. Desiring to see the world, he embarked on a self-funded mission to the Near East. Stanley ended that adventure penniless and unaccomplished, but still resolved to experience exotic locales and make a living writing about them. He offered his services to the *New York Herald*, claiming he could scoop competitors for the first story about a recent British excursion into Abyssinia. Stanley, through his intrepidness, cleverness, and luck, attached himself to the expedition and reported the story before any other journalist. In the process, he acquired the reputation of a resourceful correspondent who could deliver from distant and dangerous locations. That characteristic set him on a course for the Livingstone assignment that later brought him global fame. His subsequent transit of central Africa proved him to be more than just a reporter who stumbled upon good stories—he was then the world's preeminent explorer.

His successes and fame caught the attention of King Leopold, who sought Stanley to direct the association's efforts in Congo. But Leopold did not want Stanley as a mere figurehead. Stanley was needed because of his capacity to lead both Europeans and Africans. Few white men had spent more time exploring the region than Stanley, and none better understood how to operate in areas far from easy resupply. Stanley was a highly competent administrator who could manage workers of every background, an essential trait for expeditions that required support from dozens if not hundreds of men and women from a multitude of backgrounds. Despite claims in the English press that he was abusive of natives, Stanley adopted Livingstone's view of the importance of good relations with Africans. During his 1874 expedition, for example, he and three white companions were accompanied by 224 African men, women, and children.[15] Following their arrival on the Atlantic Coast, Stanley insisted that the *New York Herald* arrange for transport to return his African companions back to Zanzibar, writing "I cannot leave my people until the affair is settled, [and] will not."[16] While Stanley would have preferred to work for an American or English operation, he accepted Leopold's offer under the misperception that such work would help improve the region for its inhabitants and the outside world.

Stanley's first objective was to establish regular trade access to Congo. Previous association efforts favored a route from the east. Arab traders regularly dispatched caravans from the Indian Ocean to Africa's interior in search of ivory and slaves. Duplicating this approach, the Belgians established a small post on the shores of Lake Tanganyika. But the position was difficult to defend and supply. Stanley opined that an approach from the west would be superior. The Congo River was a natural pathway into this dark part of the map, but its exploitation was not without obstacles. While the course of the river is over a thousand miles, it becomes unnavigable only one hundred miles from the Atlantic Coast due to a series of impassable cataracts. Stanley's proposed solution was to establish a chain of trading stations to allow for commerce around the rapids until a railroad might be constructed alongside the river. Such a plan of action would make the enterprise profitable (morally, in Stanley's view; economically, in Leopold's opinion) while also deterring any claims to the territory by sovereign states that might seek to trump the rights of the association.

Life at these new trading posts was highly dangerous. The threat of death from attack (by man or animal), drowning (in the river or from floods), and, of course, disease (of which there were near endless varieties) was constant. Remuneration for this perilous work was less than excessive. The association offered potential station managers a mere £400 per year (about $65,000 in 2025). Accordingly, Stanley had a difficult time recruiting good men for these posts. This included Vivi, the most critical of all the stations because it was situated at the last point of navigable river in Lower Congo. Constructed on a ridge overlooking a narrow landing beach (Stanley described it as "our Acropolis"), Vivi presented a deceptively appealing front.[17] Fruit trees surrounded a series of structures designed to house officers, locals, and traders, who enjoyed a sweeping view of the river below. Vivi's station chief oversaw nearly three hundred Africans, primarily Hausas from the Gold Coast and Kabindas from Lower Congo, as well as a handful of European noncommissioned officers who were notoriously incompetent.[18] Unfortunately for Stanley,

Vivi was plagued with shoddy leadership and low morale. Writing days after one of Vivi's officers suicided, Stanley mused, "what is wanted is a strong and efficient officer of note and years, able during my absence to manage the ever intractable Europeans at Vivi. Until he comes I must have patience."[19] In March 1883, Stanley selected Duverge to run the station at Vivi. Just a month later, Duverge informed Washington that "a new Belgian company has opened trade" in the region, staffed by "Stanley's lieutenants." The association had been operating in Congo in various forms for four years at this point, so Duverge's report, in addition to failing to announce that he was joining Stanley's ranks, was somewhat misleading.

When exactly Duverge first encountered Stanley is unknown. Years later, Duverge claimed he had met Stanley when participating in the 1871–1872 Livingstone expedition. Stanley's journals make no mention of Duverge's presence before or during the search for Livingstone, an event that has been scrutinized thoroughly for over a century and a half. It is possible the two might have crossed paths during the Anglo-Ashanti War of 1873 (the conflict in which Duverge attempted to enlist while malingering in Accra). Both men were in the region at the same time. But Stanley's writings from this period make no mention of Duverge, and shortly after his arrival in the region, Duverge returned to sea. Therefore, it is highly doubtful that their first encounter was along the Gold Coast. The first documented meeting of Stanley and Duverge was in 1882 when Stanley visited Loanda for medical care. His journals record that Stanley hosted an event where he entertained several Europeans before departing from Loanda. Duverge was in attendance.

Whenever Duverge and Stanley eventually met, they likely immediately recognized some shared acquaintances. The principal benefactors of both Duverge and Stanley traveled in similar professional and social circles. Duverge's primary supporters, Paddleford and Agnus, would have known James Gordon Bennet Jr., publisher of the *New York Herald*, Stanley's old employer. In addition to being a fellow publisher, Bennet shared with Paddleford and Agnus a passion for yachting. It seems highly likely that if Bennet had ever discussed Africa with them, both Stanley and Duverge would have been mentioned in that conversation. Stanley and Duverge must also have noted similarities in their own lives. Both had fought in the Civil War. Both had lived in New York City in the late 1870s. Barely a year apart in age, both were immigrants who shared an insatiable need for adventure, particularly in Africa. It is no wonder that when sound leadership was required in one of Congo's most important outposts, Stanley found just the man in the Mauritian-born American consul.

While an announcement of the appointment was published in the Loanda press and several European papers, Duverge kept his new position secret from his State Department colleagues, likely so he might continue to collect his consular agent salary for as long as possible, a direct violation of his obligations to both the United States government and the association. He had not yet started work for Stanley and already he was lying.

Duverge assumed control of Vivi in July 1883, months after he promised to arrive. His unsuitability for the position emerged immediately. Stanley, traveling in the Upper Congo at the time, soon received notice of "a species of triangular disagreement" between the new station chief and his subordinates.[20] Louis Valcke, Stanley's deputy, was dispatched to sort out the matter. Valcke's arrival seemed to temper Duverge at first. But the new American with the French accent was never one to hold in his anger for very long, especially when someone challenged his perceived

Contemporary engraving of the Station of Vivi in the Congo Free State (1887) in Royal Museum for Central Africa, Terveuren. Public domain.

authority. A witness recorded that during dinner with several association officers, Duverge became drunk, and declared that he was not subordinate to Valcke. Duverge then "hurled a volley of insults and rudeness at him," and "during the ensuing altercation, Valcke received a slap." Valcke threatened a suit against Duverge. Duverge sent him a written apology a few days later, resolving that particular issue.[21] Other misconduct soon emerged, next from Duverge's own deputy at Vivi.

Eyre Massey Shaw Jr. was the son of the chief of London's Fire Brigade. The senior Shaw was well-known for having introduced a number of modern firefighting techniques to the fire service, including the use of metal helmets. Gilbert and Sullivan included a reference to elder Shaw's firefighting skills in their 1882 comic opera *Iolanthe*, and nine years later, Queen Victoria knighted him. No doubt attempting to compete with that legacy, the younger Shaw joined Stanley's lieutenants in Congo. There, Shaw certainly expected to encounter hardship, though perhaps not from his own supervisor.

On September 22, 1883, Shaw wrote to Stanley directly, advising that Duverge was engendering discontent at all levels in Vivi. Relations between himself and Duverge had been abysmal from the start. Discussing how Duverge had commenced his tenure by threatening Shaw, he opined, "I saw at once what kind of man he was, and that he merely wished to show me that he was too <u>smart</u> to stand any humbug." Soon after, Duverge swore at Shaw "in the presence of several Europeans and a number of negroes." Shaw offered that Duverge saw disobedience everywhere, when, in actuality, this was a consequence of his inability to properly communicate orders. "Duverge's English is so bad," wrote Shaw, "and his manner of explaining himself very often [is] so ambiguous that it is impossible for me to avoid mistaking him occasionally." Considering Duverge's shortcomings as a leader, Shaw stated, "I have simply attributed them to the want of good education, breeding, and manners." Summing up, he wrote, "Captain Duverge has no tact whatsoever in dealing with white men, and by his extraordinary conduct toward the Hausas of the Station, he has already proved that he is unfit to command negroes."[22]

By now, Stanley's deputy Valcke was back at Leopold station, the first station above the falls after Vivi, attending to more important matters. Fortunately for Stanley, Sir Frederick John Goldsmid, a former British general, was available to assist. The association had sent Goldsmid to act as something of an inspector general. He was to review Stanley's progress and report back to Brussels on the shortcomings and needs of the mission. Stanley held Goldsmid in high regard and asked the retired soldier to assess the situation at Vivi.

Goldsmid arrived in October and promptly reported that Duverge was indeed failing. He did not immediately, however, call for Duverge's removal. Regarding the dispute with Valcke, Goldsmid wrote that the matter was troublesome but now largely settled. And as for the complaints from personnel at Vivi, Goldsmid cautiously deferred to Duverge and his claim that the complaints were invalid. What troubled Goldsmid was an event that transpired shortly before his arrival in Vivi. In addition to Duverge's assault against Valcke and his insults toward Shaw and other employees, the new station chief had engaged in a gunfight with African employees of the association. The exact circumstances of the incident were unclear, but Goldsmid felt confident enough to ascribe responsibility for the dispute to Duverge's poor judgment: "Such a serious outcome . . . might have been avoided . . . had the Chief of Vivi [Duverge] not gone himself at night among a number of noisy, drunken people."

The shootout resulted in two Kabindas killed and several wounded, including Duverge, who was shot through the hand. Infuriated, all of the station's Kabindas, some of Vivi's most valuable local personnel, deserted. An alternative account of this event, highly favorable to Duverge, was published in 1890 in "Les Belges dans l'Afrique Centrale," by explorer Adolphe Burdo. According to Burdo:

> The black personnel employed at Vivi, seventy-five Kabindas and two hundred Hausa, had risen in open revolt against the white superintendent. The administrator of Vivi, Mr. Rathier-Duverge, of French origin, became agent of the Association after having fulfilled for some time the functions of United States Consul in Saint-Paul de Loanda. He defended himself valiantly with some Zanzibaris against the insurgents armed with guns and ammunition. There was an intense fight, bloodshed; three Kabindas fell under the revolver shots of Mr. Rathier-Duverge, who thus made his enemies pay dearly for the mutilation of his left hand shot through by a round.[23]

"Les Belges dans l'Afrique Centrale"

"Les Belges dans l'Afrique Centrale" is not an impartial source. The series was a compendium of narratives that uncritically related Belgian initiatives in Africa. The intended audience was readers who wanted to learn about the accomplishments of King Leopold's questionable project in Congo. Objectivity and accuracy were second to the sensationalism and patriotism that fueled sales of the books. Accordingly, the publisher admonished Burdo's early accounts for failing to properly applaud the association's successes, heavily editing his work before publishing a final version years later. It is reasonable to conclude that the final version is more fiction than fact.

In reality, Duverge was an incompetent leader. The remaining staff at Vivi were in a state of paralysis because of his overbearing and unpredictable command. Goldsmid, though, still resisted asking Stanley to terminate Duverge. Instead, he departed for other inspections, hoping to return to Vivi in a few weeks and find the station in a better condition.

Duverge's behavior, however, remained unacceptable.

In October, Duverge and some men from Vivi seized the key town of Boma. Claimed by the Portuguese but in an area disputed by several powers, Boma was home to Belgian, French, Portuguese, and Dutch trading houses. Four years earlier, Stanley had described the town's history as "two centuries of pitiless persecution of black men by sordid whites."[24] Boma was one of several locations the association was seeking to peel away from the influence of the European powers, especially France, whose Italian-born explorer Pierre Savorgnan de Brazza was hard at work undermining Stanley's efforts. The association would formally negotiate to acquire the town the following year, but apparently Duverge could not wait for diplomacy. Instead, he arrived in Boma, firing into the air before hoisting the association's flag over the town. He then imprisoned a native chief, demanding, according to a witness, "a substantial ransom." When money was not forthcoming, Duverge finally accepted "one of the man's three daughters." Reportedly, the young lady spent the night with Duverge in a French warehouse before Duverge and his men returned to Vivi, considering their Boma mission a success.

When Goldsmid learned of this unsanctioned attempt at annexation, he demanded an explanation. Duverge claimed he had been headed to check on a steamer that was reportedly downstream without a captain or pilot when he happened to pass through Boma. Seeing an opportunity to claim the town for the association before land speculators made the territory unaffordable, he seized the place on his own initiative. He made no mention in his explanation of why it was necessary to imprison a local chief, much less one of his daughters. This sort of incomplete answer was standard for Duverge, but Goldsmid's military sensibilities would have none of it. The general put the question to Duverge directly: "Did he, or did he not, in his capacity as a representative of the International Association for the Congo, imprison [the chief] and did he accept one of the prisoner's daughters as a condition of his release?" Duverge responded that he had not. His accusers were "conspirators and liars," and time would eventually show he was the innocent party. He then resigned.[25]

Thus concluded Duverge's brief service as an agent of the association.

Both Goldsmid and Stanley were charitable to Duverge in their public accounts. The London papers reported that Duverge had resigned "on account of his having become embroiled with the natives," with no further details.[26] Privately, Goldsmid informed Stanley that Duverge had been a complete failure, noting that in addition to the poor leadership, gunfights, and abduction of locals, Duverge had been negotiating treaties on his own accord. Those efforts complicated Stanley's attempts to reach agreements with the local tribes (an effort, unbeknownst to Stanley at the time, that was already being undermined by secret representatives from Belgium, particularly Goldsmid).

Stanley never wrote "Duverge" in any of his published journals, describing his Vivi hire only as "V." and "Captain V.", presumably to avoid the potentiality of a defamation suit. But it was clear from his descriptions that Duverge was the subject of his disappointment. Reflecting several years later on the achievements of Shaw, who became Duverge's successor, Stanley framed those accomplishments in the light of Duverge's exceptionally poor performance:

> Mr. E. Massey Shaw, of London, deserves honourable mention at
> my hands for some months of excellent governorship of Yivi [Vivi]
> during a term which, I fear, gave him more pain and anxiety than
> comfort or pleasure. For his sturdy, calm conduct under distressing
> circumstances, this hearty acknowledgment is due him. We had been
> unfortunate enough to have accepted the services of an applicant
> who, through an alleged long term of service in the United States
> Navy formerly, and latterly as American consul at St. Paul de Loanda,
> was supposed to be well worthy of this important appointment. If
> one may judge by results, a very serious error was committed by me
> when I accepted this person and appointed him to Yivi [Vivi]. After
> a short, but disastrous term, he was dismissed. To repair the many
> in Africa mischiefs resulting from mismanagement, and to restore
> confidence in the minds of the panic-stricken natives and frightened
> employees, was a task which fell to his successor, Mr. Shaw.[27]

Clearly, Stanley was genuinely angered by Duverge's methods of command. Still laboring under the notion that he was in Congo to promote progressive ideals like eradicating slavery and opening the region to free commerce, Stanley was shocked by Duverge's propensity for violence and intolerance of native authorities. That cruelty and Stanley's naivety accurately foreshadow the region's tragic future.

In 1884, Chancellor Bismarck hosted the Berlin Conference to discuss the division of Africa among the major powers. Unlike other European states, Belgium did not press for new territory. Instead, King Leopold emphasized that while his International Association of the Congo was already realizing great success under the guidance of the esteemed Henry Morton Stanley, more could be achieved if he were granted exclusive authority over the region. Leopold underlined that this authority was sought so that he could act as a benevolent administrator of the region, not a colonial ruler.

The Belgian king offered an appealing alternative to the usual carving up of the African continent. The seemingly enlightened Leopold pledged to continue introducing open and fair commerce to Congo while simultaneously indoctrinating the local population with the benefits of Christendom and European civilization. He would fund the state using only his personal wealth, establishing a new government composed of capable Europeans, principally Belgians, who would negotiate honest and mutually beneficial agreements with native tribes. Leopold would hold Congo as his personal possession, entirely separate from the nation of Belgium.

The attendees of the conference supported the proposal. Leopold achieved this support partly because the major powers wished to prevent a rival from gaining control of Congo. It was far better, from the perspective of both London and Paris, that tiny Belgium controlled Congo rather than a larger state. Altruism was also a sincere factor in the agreement. A multitude of what today would be termed nongovernmental organizations, mostly religious groups and societal improvement associations, embraced Leopold's claims that he would administer the region benevolently. They then urged their governments to agree to the terms of the Berlin Conference. It was hoped that Leopold would oversee a new type of state, one founded on principles of free trade and fair treatment of the indigenous population. Leopold's insistence that he would eradicate slavery in the region appealed to abolitionists who had won their cause at home but still saw battles to be fought abroad. This was particularly true in Africa, where indigenous chiefs and Arab merchants were still heavily engaged in the trade. The newly established "Congo Free State," like the International Association of the Congo before it, was to promote the welfare of the native peoples in the region and open Congo to the benefit of the entire world, not just the mercantile aims of a single foreign power. The pitch was successful.

Writing four years after its establishment, Henry Phillips Jr. of Philadelphia's American Philosophical Society characterized the early Congo Free State as such:

The creation of the Congo Independent state may be considered as one of the most curious and most characteristic episodes of the nineteenth century. All settlements formerly made in unexplored countries were the results of missionary labors, or of wealth or fame seeking adventurers. Motives of policy on the part of European governments then came into play to facilitate the reduction and colonization of the new-found lands. To no such causes was the founding of the Congo Independent state indebted, neither religious fervor nor thirst of gold caused it to see the light. The philanthropy of the King of the Belgians, together with his love of geographical explorations, were to be the means of pouring light of civilization upon "the dark continent."[28]

By European estimations, Congo required just such an intervention. The place was riddled with un-Christian and uncivilized behavior. Duverge's predecessor at Vivi, Jozef Van de Velde, opined: "While I was at Vivi, the King of Yella died and someone came to tell me that they were going to immolate three slaves to be buried with him." Van de Velde was appalled, and endeavored to stop the sacrifices. He declared that the deceased chief was his ally and should therefore be "buried as a white man." After sending the tribe a coffin and honor guard, Van de Velde noted that "subsequent deaths have been met by the . . . natives forgoing sacrifices. I am convinced that the barbaric custom of human sacrifice, unfortunately common in the Congo State, will disappear as the circle of action of the stations increases."[29]

There was some reason, then, to believe that Leopold's project might truly help the people of Congo. Tragically though, the Congo Free State's successes in curtailing slavery and growing trade were later eclipsed by an unreserved, blood-soaked race for government-subsidized profit. To administer his massive new territory more efficiently, Leopold granted a series of authorities to European overseers and local collaborators who were more like Duverge than Stanley. Their actions were often unconscionable. What had started as an experiment to improve and help a land perceived as uncivilized and backward developed into a rapacious, heartless system designed to exploit the region's resources at any cost, without consideration for traditional customs or governance. Initially, ivory was the principal target of this system. But eventually rubber, because of the growing demand for bicycle tires and its industrial use, became the main source of wealth from Congo.

In 1886, Leopold formed the Force Publique, a gendarme service that administered his rule in Congo. The Force Publique's complement varied, but generally included between two hundred and four hundred European officers and five thousand to twenty-five thousand native troops, depending on the year and political circumstances. Like Leopold's other regional efforts, this element at first promoted progressive goals. The Force Publique warred against Arab slave traders in eastern Congo and acted as a police force in the country's settled areas. But Congo's real wealth was situated away from the narrow strip along the Congo River where European traders attempted to spark commerce.

Rubber plantations were the actual driver of the Free State's economy. As demand for rubber grew in the late nineteenth century, the need to cultivate remote areas of Congo required a further devolution of authority to lower levels. While initially Leopold had controlled Congo from trading stations on the river, he now passed power to fiefdoms throughout the interior. As his limited oversight diminished, abuses increased. From the Belgian king's perspective, his project was a success. Congo generated tremendous wealth Leopold used to construct museums and other enlightened projects in Belgium.

On the ground in the Congo Free State, though, unscrupulous concessionaires were grossly abusing local inhabitants to generate more and more profit. Soon, the Force Publique was actively involved in maintaining rubber quotas by suppressing the inevitable resistance to this rule. Natives were beaten, tortured, and killed for failing to produce enough rubber, as Congo descended into a plantation state. When they were not assaulting the local population, the Force Publique kept busy hunting wild game, which was abundant in the region. But ammunition was expensive. To prevent this unnecessary cost, soldiers were instructed to only discharge their weapons when attacked by resisting natives. To demonstrate that they had actually been attacked, troops were instructed to produce the hand of any African they shot. Force Publique soldiers who harvested a sufficient number of hands were awarded with extra pay or early release from their tour in Congo. Inevitably, the conduct of the Force Publique, composed of mercenaries and individuals with a character similar to Duverge, degenerated into near-unchecked criminality. The Europeans and their African proxy soldiers lobbed off the hands of innocent locals, including those of children. Estimates of the number of people killed in the Congo Free State reached as high as ten million. If Leopold was not actively suborning genocide, he certainly did little to prevent something that looked similar to such a crime.

Duverge's small gunfight in Vivi seems benign relative to these later horrors. But at the time, three years before the start of the Force Publique's gruesome campaign, Duverge's removal from Congo engendered some attention outside of Stanley's camp. Days after his wounding, Consul General Francis in Lisbon, still technically Duverge's State Department superior as Duverge had not yet resigned his consular commission, was summoned to the Portuguese Foreign Ministry. There the Foreign Minister advised:

> His majesty's government had learned of the presence of the American consul in the upper Congo and of his activity with Stanley in the aggressive war of the latter upon certain chiefs who are friendly to the Portuguese and to their rule in the territory now overrun by Stanley, and is claimed as the rightful possession of Portugal, that in a recent fight by Stanley with the natives, the consul who was assisting the latter was seriously wounded.[30]

The minister characterized Duverge's activities as a "disagreeable incident" he could not believe had the sanction of the United States, a sentiment no doubt shared by Consul General Francis and his peers at the State Department.[31] Years later, Duverge remembered the incident differently, offering that he had "saved the lives of the French missionaries whom the negroes were going to kill" and that he "was decorated with the Legion of Honor."[32] This was untrue, of course. Duverge never saved any missionaries, nor did he ever receive the Legion of Honor. His inept management of the Vivi station was unsurprising in light of his history. In virtually every role Duverge had taken—French soldier, first mate, American officer, consular agent, trading post manager—he had failed by some measure because of overconfidence in himself. And when Duverge became aware of his inadequacies, his tendency was violence.

THE CONGO EXPEDITION.

LISBON, SEPTEMBER 18.

Intelligence, dated August 18, has reached here from the Congo by the Portuguese mail steamer that Mr. Stanley was expected to return to the West Coast. There was no news of the arrival of Major-general Sir Frederick Goldsmith, whose advent in the Congo region on a special mission from the King of the Belgians would, it was thought, create a surprise. It was reported that Mr. Stanley was at the International Association's station at Vivi. Among the passengers who have arrived here by this steamer are Lieutenant Vandervelde and M. Sigismond Back, who belonged to Mr. Stanley's expedition. Mr. Duverge, former American Consul at Loando, is now serving with the expedition. The report of the death of Captain Janssens, who, while acting on Mr. Stanley's behalf, was attacked by natives in the interior, is confirmed. It appears that M. de Brazza is about to establish a station at Chiloango, over which Portugal claims sovereignty. The French have burnt a few native huts in a small village of Loango ; but this affair is described as a common incident in the country, to which no importance is attached. M. de Brazza has had a cordial interview in the interior with Mr. Elliot.

Duverge's arrival in Congo, and later misconduct, was noted as far away as in the European press. Birmingham Daily Post, September 19, 1878

Following his ejection from Vivi, Duverge found himself back in Banana, still technically the U.S. consular agent in Loanda. From there he sent one of his last communications as a U.S. diplomat. Responding to the queries Consular General John Francis had sent from Lisbon months before about the Silveira brothers, Duverge wrote that the case was hopeless. Duverge then added an entirely irrelevant missive about the Portuguese slave trade.

In Angola where the slave trade still exists, there is no Law nor Justice. I have followed that accursed from Loanda to near Bihe, and from Loanda to San Salvador and as far as Stanley Pool. I have new proof which will be exhibited to the U.S. Govt on my return home where I am going by leave of absence granted me from [the] State Department and dated August 27, 1883. My health is so poor that I hardly know if I'll ever reach the State [sic], but hope that God will grant it.

Duverge's final official message was his resignation, mailed from Liverpool in January 1884. Washington accepted it without comment. Duverge's days as a diplomat were behind him. His next adventure awaited: Madagascar.

CHAPTER FOUR

The Cemetery of Europeans

In addition to sending a resignation letter to the State Department, Duverge wrote Vice-Consul Newton in Loanda, to whom he returned the consulate's papers and seals. Duverge sent no communication to his wife in New York. After a year had passed, a mutual acquaintance informed her that Duverge was alive and in Liverpool. Mrs. Duverge's response to this news was to serve her husband with a summons for divorce proceedings, grounding her petition in the claim that "between the time of her marriage and when she went to Africa, her husband . . . proved unfaithful to her on various occasions." Likely to put pressure on him to settle quickly, she shared her understanding of Duverge's life with the *New York Times*: "Duverge is from an ancient French family. Being born in America, from his youth he took part in its politics. The love of travel was born in him, and while still a young man, he footed it with great perseverance through the wilderness of Asia and Africa, made a walking tour through the greater part of the European continent, and was with Stanley through the latter's celebrated trip through the 'Dark Continent.'"[1]

All of this is exaggeration and lies, except for his love of travel.

The divorce summons arrived in England too late. Duverge had left Liverpool in July, bound for Madagascar. He was not alone. As the American consul in Madagascar explained in a note to the State Department, "The late discovery of rich gold deposits, together with the supposed other good openings for adventurers made by the war, is already attracting all sorts of characters to the country and they will rapidly increase. Among them will be found many disreputable characters."[2]

Duverge was one of those characters. Multiple sources recorded his arrival. In August, a contact of the American consul reported:

> The landing of a man at Mananjary, a port some 300 miles south of this [Tamatave, Madagascar]. It seems that this man is, or has been, in our Consular service. There is a Mauritian gentleman residing in this town who was at Mananjary at the time this notable warrior landed there, and he has described him to me as he appeared the day after landing. He was, said my informant, on a horse some resident had loaned him; was dressed in a fantastic Eastern costume, had an enormous sword buckled to his side, and two horse pistols stuck in the belt. In reply to my informant's question as to the object of his invasion, he said, with an air of deep mystery and serious importance, that his mission was a secret one, and that he was going to march on the capital—when there would be a great change in the state of things! It is to be hoped that if he successfully endures the fatigue of the long march to the capital under the weight of all those arms and titles, he will neither frighten the Queen and her government out of the capital, nor massacre all the French forces, should it be his fortune to meet them,—I hear that he carries the U.S. flag.[3]

An article in the island's English language newspaper also recorded the landing, including the text of Duverge's card that credited him as a member of the Société de Géographie. Also noted was that he had arrived with "French bulldogs."[4] Captain Samuel P. Oliver,[5] then a British military observer, as well witnessed Duverge's arrival in Madagascar: "On the day following the last bombardment of Mahanoro a vessel, The *Coleridge*, hailing from Mauritius, put into Mananzary [Manajary], where an American, styling himself Captain and Brevet-Major L. de R. du Vergé and U.S. consul for St. Paul de Loanda and south-west coast of Africa, landed with a staff of two secretaries, five companions and a servant. This small party proceeded to Antananarivo, but the object of their mission has not yet transpired."[6]

The object of Duverge's mission was fortune-seeking.

Madagascar was in the midst of the first Franco-Hova War, France's initial attempt to seize power from the Hova government that controlled most of the island. The outcome of that conflict was, at the time, undetermined. French Marines had successfully landed along parts of Madagascar's north and northwestern coasts. Tamatave, the country's major port, was under siege from the French Navy.[7] But the Hova government had some reason to be optimistic. The country's capital of Antananarivo, deep inside the island's interior, was safe from any immediate attack. Additionally, the Malagasy Army remained largely intact and motivated to fight. French forces, meanwhile, were suffering low morale, fighting in a distant land in a war that lacked strong support from home. The Hovas sensed an opportunity to counterattack, force a French withdrawal, and secure Antananarivo's rule over the entire island. The Hovas also understood that foreign help would be needed.

Duverge's arrival was in answer to that call. He was not in Madagascar to spread Christianity or educate the island's children or make peace between competing European interests. He was there adventuring: searching for wealth, influence, and fame. However, he and his newly landed entourage did not depart for the capital immediately. Duverge spent two weeks at the east coast port of Mahanoro, penning flattering letters to governmental leaders in Antananarivo. He had no real interest in whether the Hova government stood or fell but, as a student of the region, knew that his best chance for a quick fortune was in the palace. And as a lifelong sycophant, Duverge understood that toadying and self-promotion might earn him an audience. It was a smart bet. After gaining a letter of introduction from the regional governor, Duverge set out directly for the capital. Somewhere along the way, one of his secretaries abandoned the group "because of poor treatment by Duverge."[8] Yet another hire who could not tolerate Duverge and his temper.

On October 5, 1884, Duverge met with Prime Minister Rainilaiarivony, a brilliant statesman, administrator, politician, and military commander, precisely the sort of acquaintance Duverge aimed to cultivate. Rainilaiarivony's father, prime minister and consort to Queen Ranavalona I, had died in 1852. The queen suggested at that time to the then-twenty-four-year-old Rainilaiarivony that he should replace his father as consort. Rainilaiarivony respectfully declined the offer, instead committing himself to helping the queen conquer Madagascar's southern and western regions, which were still largely free of Hova domination.

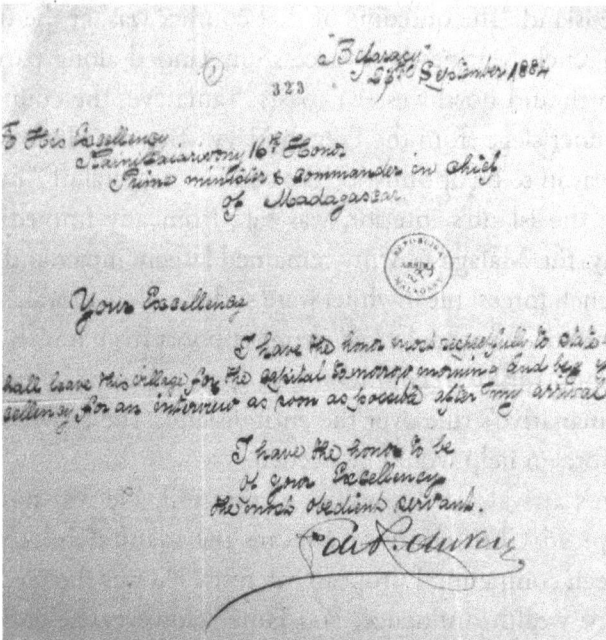

Duverge writes to Prime Minister Rainilaiarivony, National Archives, Republic of Madagascar.

During this period, Rainilaiarivony sided with the queen against a succession of coups, cementing his position as a trusted advisor.

After Queen Ranavalona I's death, her son ruled briefly before Queen Rasoherina took the throne in 1864. Valuing his reputation as a loyalist, Rainilaiarivony was invited to be the new queen's consort, an offer similar to the one he had declined twelve years earlier. This time, however, perhaps because his father had not had relations with this particular queen, he accepted. Rainilaiarivony was intent on ruling, though, not just marrying into power. Under his instruction, Queen Rasoherina vested him with authorities as both the prime minister and commander in chief of the army. He would hold those positions for three decades and through three queens, serving as consort to each. Throughout that time, various monarchs retained their image of authority, but Rainilaiarivony was undoubtedly the most significant figure of Malagasy political life. The prime minister implemented a host of reforms during his tenure. He organized the government into specific competencies, initiated infrastructure improvements, sought uniformity in taxation, encouraged

Hova colonization of non-Hova territories, Christianized the court, developed a Western system of law and education, and greatly modernized the army. He frequently relied on foreigners to deliver outside expertise and assistance.

Duverge, dressed in a foreign officer's uniform and regaling the prime minister with tales of combat on three continents, must have seemed an ideal candidate to join the Hova fight. In a note sent to the prime minister after their first meeting, Duverge offered that he had "the sentiment of a soldier who is more than friendly to your cause and nation."[9] Duverge praised the Hovas and commended the prime minister and Queen Ranavalona III. He then wrote, "you have in your army an officer from one of the two friendly powers to your gov't," and suggested that the prime minister grant him "the same privilege." Duverge added that he did not wish to "supplant anyone."[10] This was Duverge's attempt to address the reality that he had arrived too late in Madagascar to receive charge of the Hova Army. That responsibility had already been vested in an Englishman, Digby Willoughby.

Digby Willoughby did things his way. When he arrived in southern Africa in 1871, he was unattached to a European military force, preferring to seek his fortune on his terms. It was not until eight years later, then in his mid-thirties, Willoughby accepted a commission as a captain in the Natal Native Contingent during the First Zulu War. The next year, he raised a group of cavalry to serve under him during the Basutoland Rebellion of 1880. Between conflicts, he spent time as an auctioneer and actor. His reputation as an officer adept at training and leading native soldiers was apparently enduring, though, because, in September 1883, the Hovas offered him command of their army. Willoughby accepted, arriving in Antananarivo in January 1884. Queen Ranavalona III named him an adjutant general and the principal military advisor to Prime Minister Rainilaiarivony, giving Willoughby a direct line to the actual decision-maker in the country. General Willoughby was granted command of the entire Hova Army, some twenty thousand men.

Six months later, Duverge appeared, begging Rainilaiarivony to appoint him to a station equal to Willoughby. Duverge implied that the Hova government had some level of obligation to give co-command of their army to an American. He was right insofar as both the British and American governments were favorably disposed toward the Hovas, albeit with different motivations. The British supported Rainilaiarivony and each queen's government out of political convenience, seeking to deny France a colony in southwestern Africa. American aims at the time, in Madagascar and nearly everywhere outside the Western hemisphere, were more economic than political. The United States promised noninterference in exchange for free trade, signing treaties to this effect with the Hovas in 1867 and 1881. U.S. consuls were deployed to support American commerce in Madagascar, and by the time of the first Franco-Hova War, America was the primary source of manufactured goods in Madagascar.

Despite Duverge's appeal, the prime minister was an experienced enough administrator to know that a functioning army could not have two supreme commanders. Accordingly, Duverge was commissioned into the Hova effort, but only as a colonel. How General Willoughby felt about the new colonel is unrecorded. Perhaps Willoughby would have welcomed the skills of a French-speaking, combat-hardened American officer who possessed familiarity with the region. Or maybe he saw Duverge for what he was: a boastful, temperamental, opportunistic rival. In any case, Duverge was now under Willoughby's command. The general set him to work.

Duverge was charged with improving fortifications, first in Antananarivo and then throughout the island. This was a curious duty for a soldier who had no previous training as an engineer or artilleryman. While Duverge likely had some experience as a sapper during the Italian Campaign, his service there would have given him only a rudimentary understanding of physical defenses. Nevertheless, between his European duties and the inevitable appreciation for fortifications that he gained during the Siege of Charleston, Duverge had more knowledge of the matter than probably any other man in Madagascar at the time. He certainly possessed a better understanding of fortifications than anyone in the Hova Army, which, though still holding its ground after a year of combat with the French, was hardly a modern fighting force. They were well equipped, however. Anticipating hostilities with the French, Rainilaiarivony had procured significant numbers of European firearms and ammunition before fighting commenced. But the army was inexperienced and poorly disciplined. Willoughby observed that when he first arrived in Madagascar, the Hovas disorganized "under the ridiculous impression that it was possible for a shell to travel sixty or seventy miles."[11] Duverge's knowledge might have been limited, but it was the best they had.

For the next four months, Duverge traveled throughout Madagascar, advising the Hova Army on how to better protect itself from French attacks. One observer recorded that the

> fortifications constructed by the Hovas were very simple and very comfortable. This was the inventiveness of Captain Duverge. The entryways for the cannons were carved out of the hill so that the recesses and the earth into which they were pulled back served to conceal the battlements in such a way that they were entirely protected from the shots coming from the river. In the less elevated places he filled baskets with earth and stones so that the cannon was [sheltered] in its battlement.[12]

Never one to stick to his assigned tasks, he sent lengthy missives to Antananarivo, demanding that the army employ better prophylactic measures to guard against illness. Sick himself throughout most of his time in Madagascar, Duverge insisted that his own troops take care against what he deemed an unhealthy climate, even though it was the only environment the Hova fighters had ever known. Despite his griping, Duverge impressed with his basic soldiering skills and dashing uniform, usually a European suit with Hova insignia. His competence with firearms was affirmed in the commentary of Antoine Perraud, a French prisoner who observed Duverge's shooting while they were together in the countryside. "Duverge is one of the best marksmen I have ever seen. I have seen him kill a sitting duck with his precision carbine with an explosive bullet. The duck was hit, and the bullet cut right through its neck, something that I have seen with my own eyes and that I can attest to."[13]

How Corporal Perraud of the French Marines came to be attached to Colonel Louis Duverge of the Hova Army is a story in and of itself. Fortunately, one of Perraud's great-granddaughters, Marilyn O'Day, researched and shared Perraud's tale in a superbly edited 2002 narrative entitled "Escape from Madagascar: Journals of a French Marine,

1884-1887." The self-published manuscript, scrupulously translated from Perraud's notes, details Perraud's time as a Hova prisoner in Madagascar and remembrances later shared with relatives. "Escape from Madagascar" is a priceless historical text and an invaluable window into the life of Duverge during this period.

Corporal Perraud arrived in Majunga, a port city in northwest Madagascar, in July 1884, a month before Duverge landed on the opposite side of the island. Four months later, Hova warriors seized Perraud while on patrol. In later life, Perraud claimed he had been captured, showing scars as proof he was taken against his will. However, internal Malagasy documents and comments from Duverge strongly suggest Perraud deserted, a process that did not go entirely as planned. During his desertion, Perraud was speared, an injury which kept him incapacitated for several months. Perraud recovered under the care of Hova guards, who moved him from camp to camp in Madagascar's interior as they awaited orders from Antananarivo about what to do with him. Duverge arrived before the orders. Officially charged with improving Hova fortifications, Duverge was carrying out his Malagasy military obligations with the same approach he had taken with his American diplomatic duties. Duverge executed his assigned work but concurrently explored the countryside, apparently out of personal curiosity. While doing so, he learned of the captured Frenchman and hurried to Perraud's location. Duverge offered the young corporal a deal: become Duverge's servant and he would release Perraud once the two of them were back in Antananarivo. Perraud, after months of fevers and a lingering spear wound, wished nothing more than to escape Madagascar. He immediately accepted Duverge's offer. He would remain by Duverge's side until March 1886. Duverge, perhaps because Perraud was a native French speaker or maybe because of their shared French military affiliation, became very close to Perraud—and loquacious. Perraud clandestinely recorded many of their conversations in a cryptic shorthand that, thankfully, his descendants could and did interpret. His description of his first meeting with Duverge is notable: "He was wearing gray flannel pants a la demi-Turk, held in at his knees by good gray-black wool stockings, serving as gaiters. This garb fit him well. The little vest that he wore did not button and was adorned with five pockets on each side: one for his watch, one for a thermometer, a barometer, pedometer, and compass. When he came to converse with me, he struck me as being a good man."[14]

Here, months into his exploration of the Malagasy hinterlands, Duverge carries himself as more of a wandering geographer than a campaigning soldier. Whether he was trying to influence officials in Washington or African tribesmen, Duverge knew the power of image. This frequently led to him assuming unassigned roles.

Willoughby had ordered Duverge to improve Hova fortifications. Duverge did so, but simultaneously worked to establish a détente between the Sakalava tribes, who inhabited much of the ungoverned west coast, and the Hova government. Only after he had commenced these negotiations did Duverge write to Rainilaiarivony to inform him that efforts were underway to establish a truce between the Antananarivo and key Sakalava leaders. Duverge boasted that he could arrange for chiefs of the region to submit to the Hovas "without bloodshed," warning that any attempt to conquer the natives in that region would be dangerous since they had paid "white men" with "gold dust" to train them how to fight. He shared that he had animosity against all enemies of "the true Malagasy cause and perfect independence of Madagascar against any foreign foes, but most particularly against those confounded 'Red coats' of English."[15] The reaction from the prime minister was lukewarm, but he allowed Duverge to continue. And so he did, often finding success. As an American, Duverge presented himself to the Sakalavas as an objective outsider. The French were there to steal the island and take its resources. The English were there to preach, counter the French, and perhaps take Madagascar themselves. The Americans merely offered high-quality, reasonably priced consumer goods. Duverge advocated for Queen Ranavalona's government, arguing to the Sakalavas that the Hovas were necessary if the French were to be expelled, the English muted, and the Americans encouraged to trade. In many cases, this approach worked. Though Madagascar's tribes had been fighting for centuries, Duverge managed to achieve a level of ecumenical understanding between some of the most important Sakalava chiefs and the Hova government, establishing important relationships that Antananarivo could use to defend the country against European encroachment. But Duverge's ultimate objective was not the continued independence of Madagascar. On the contrary, Perraud records that Duverge was thinking only of himself:

> Duverge was being farsighted. He confided the following to me: to become acquainted with the Sakalave chiefs in this area, and in making friends with these men, he could use them either for or against the Hovas. In the case where the Hovas were not working to his advantage, he would unite the Sakalaves, and they would rebel against the Hova government. This would give him the chance to trade along the Sakalave coasts and to have for a protector the French Government, who currently was his enemy. Everything was well thought out and the politics that Duverge employed were sly and twofaced, for this man was capable of doing anything for money, and always found himself on the side that paid him the best.[16]

As Duverge worked to improve Hova relations and capabilities in the countryside, Willoughby continued his efforts with the Hova Army. Regular training and drilling of the troops were central to these efforts. Heightened discipline was also imperative. When two men were caught deserting, Willoughby had them shot. Later, he fused English discipline with Malagasy methods, forcing the entire army to take an oath accepting that "any soldier convicted of cowardice on the field of battle should be burnt alive."[17] Queen Ranavalona's army was soon a capable fighting force. In February 1885, the American consul described the mood in the palace as "resolved and sanguine" as the Hovas prepared their counteroffensive.[18] Duverge reported on March 22 that he and his men were in position to "watch well the movements of the French."[19] Willoughby then launched an attack on the already encircled Tamatave, which France had seized early in the war.

The town had been decimated by a year of warfare. Malaria was rampant. Resupply of food and medicine was limited to small boats launched from French naval vessels. The American consul saw France's prospects as bleak, noting they had not "gained a step towards the conquest of the Hovas, or towards bringing them to agree to cede the North-West coast, or any other part of the island."[20] Willoughby's attack increased the pressure. Paris's toehold on Madagascar was slipping.

Desperate in September, the French attempted to break out of Tamatave. Willoughby's men met them fiercely, protected by Duverge's fortifications. An observer described that the Malagasy forces seemed "to be covered with extensive intrenchments from base to summit," allowing the Hovas to safely drive back the attack.[21] The French retreated to Tamatave. In October, convinced that subjugation of the entire island would be too costly, Paris agreed to peace talks. French naval officers commenced negotiations with the Hova's designated representative: General Willoughby. But Willoughby was a better general than he was a diplomat. He failed to uphold Malagasy interests and gave in readily to French demands. After a peace treaty was signed in January 1886, French negotiators commented, "the English adventurer served us well in this affair."[22]

Duverge retreated to Antananarivo in July, claiming illness. There, he wrote to Prime Minister Rainilaiarivony for assistance. Duverge understood that Queen Ranavalona had "a great number of slaves." He thought that several might be provided to help him carry "water, mail, and myself when required." Former Union officer Duverge opined that these slaves would "save me one great deal of trouble in my present state of ill health."[23] In addition to trying to procure Africans to carry him around, Duverge was considering his future after the war.

In November 1885, Duverge wrote to General Willoughby's staff that he was obliged to leave the Hova Army. Duverge claimed that reports of the execution of French prisoners by the Hovas made his continued service impossible. Willoughby's deputy, fellow Englishman Charles Shervington, responded to Duverge that he was required to return to Antananarivo and render to General Willoughby in person his resignation, as well as surrender his commission and use of the title "colonel." Duverge, always officious when it suited him, asserted he could only formally resign if the queen herself requested the return of his commission. He added that he would continue to use his military title while remaining in Madagascar's countryside as an officer emeritus. Willoughby, no doubt concerned about the presence of a disillusioned officer of dubious loyalty roaming about the interior of Madagascar, negotiated an agreement whereby Prime Minister Rainilaiarivony requested Duverge's resignation on behalf of Queen Ranavalona. Duverge, balancing his desire to operate freely with a practical need to not alienate the Hovas unless absolutely necessary, agreed. He returned to Antananarivo in March 1886 to effectuate his resignation. Duverge attempted to negotiate an agreement to take Malagasy student Teodore Andrainaporio to Baltimore, where it was promised the young man would be taught how to make "torpidos, dynamites, cartridges, shells, electric lights, and batterys" and "not leave him on any account or return to Madagascar" for four months.[24] The agreement fell through after the Hova government requested a contract for the arrangement, which Duverge refused to sign, arguing that "in America my word is sufficient."[25]

When Duverge returned to the capital, he brought his French servant Perraud with him. Upon meeting Perraud, Willoughby offered to take him on as his own valet. Duverge agreed, and Perraud was soon at work for the general. Perraud did not remain with Willoughby long, however. In May 1886, a new French resident, a formal representative from Paris and a condition of the agreement Willoughby had negotiated, arrived in Antananarivo. Under the terms of the Franco-Hova treaty, the resident was empowered with broad authorities in Madagascar. Knowing that if he was found as a deserter the French might court-martial him, Perraud received Willoughby's permission to flee the island. After a circuitous journey to the East Coast, Perraud escaped Madagascar for America in August 1886.

Willoughby left Madagascar the following year. Despite his shortcomings as a diplomat in negotiating peace with the French, Queen Ranavalona dispatched the general to London to act as her ambassador. There, he spent two years promoting Malagasy causes to Foreign Office officials, who concurrently tried to sort out what to do about a British subject who claimed to be a foreign ambassador. The matter was eventually resolved when Willoughby was recalled to Antananarivo. There, he was tried for embezzlement for his lavish living expenses, including a £300 charge (approximately $55,000 in 2025) for his personal uniforms. Willoughby was convicted and sentenced to ten years' imprisonment.[26] After a brief incarceration in Antananarivo, Willoughby was granted clemency and sent to Tamatave. For nearly two weeks, he was detained there in a hut, his former soldiers his guards, until he was thrust aboard a departing steamer and banished from the country forever.[27]

Duverge also left Antananarivo. He went west, back into the hinterlands he had previously explored. Perraud later reported that Duverge might have been forced to resign and flee the capital because of suspicions about his loyalties. Speculation about Duverge emerged after a member of his entourage, M. Fontenay, defected to the French side in 1885. Fontenay, a member of Duverge's original group that had accompanied him when he first came ashore in August 1884, not only abandoned the Hovas, but gave the enemy valuable intelligence about the fortifications Duverge had been working to improve. While the Hova authorities and Willoughby certainly had reason to doubt Duverge's loyalties, there is no proof he ever worked for the French. Extensive Malagasy records demonstrate that Fontenay abandoned Duverge for the same reason so many other employees abandoned Duverge: because he was cruel. When Fontenay objected to his superior's domineering attitude, Duverge attempted to have him arrested for insubordination. When that failed, he accused Fontenay of theft, threatening him with lengthy imprisonment. At some point, Fontenay decided a better life was on the other side of the line with the French. Duverge likely left Antananarivo after the war, not because he cared about French prisoners or because he was suspected of espionage, but because he knew change was coming. Hova power was waning. While the French had failed to secure the island, it was apparent that the Hovas were ready to surrender, legally and practically, much of their authority to Paris. Always shrewd, Duverge likely saw that, in loudly decrying the supposed Hova execution of prisoners, he could pivot toward the French and perhaps benefit from their rising influence in Madagascar. An artful politician, he was careful to maintain some degree of cooperation with the Hovas. In fact, upon accepting his resignation, Queen Ranavalona granted him seventy acres of west coast land for his service.

With title to that property in hand, Duverge embarked on a personal survey of the country. For nine months he traveled clockwise around Madagascar. Starting with a visit to the Sihanakas tribe northeast of Antananarivo, he moved south to the territory of the Tanalas after he determined "I wanted to go as far as I could from the neighborhood of any Hovas, because I was afraid of them more than the vipers." From there, Duverge traveled to the central highlands and the land of the Betsileo people, where he recorded details of their complex funeral traditions and suffering under the Hova-backed slave trade. Duverge then passed time with the Antemoros of the southeast, moving along the coast from tribe to tribe before spending his final months among the Sakalava, who populated the majority of Madagascar's southwestern coastal region.

Thankfully, he recorded these travels in a book, *Madagascar and Independent Peoples: Abandoned by France,* published in Paris in 1887.[28] His work is part travelogue, part propaganda piece, part prospectus. There is no evidence that the text ever achieved any significant audience, but its recollections are an excellent insight into the man and his era, as well as Madagascar. Duverge felt, at times, that his writing skills were inadequate to explain the island to those who had not visited.

"The trees, the streams, the rivers are admirable," Duverge shared, "and together form an enchanting aspect which it is impossible for my pen to paint."

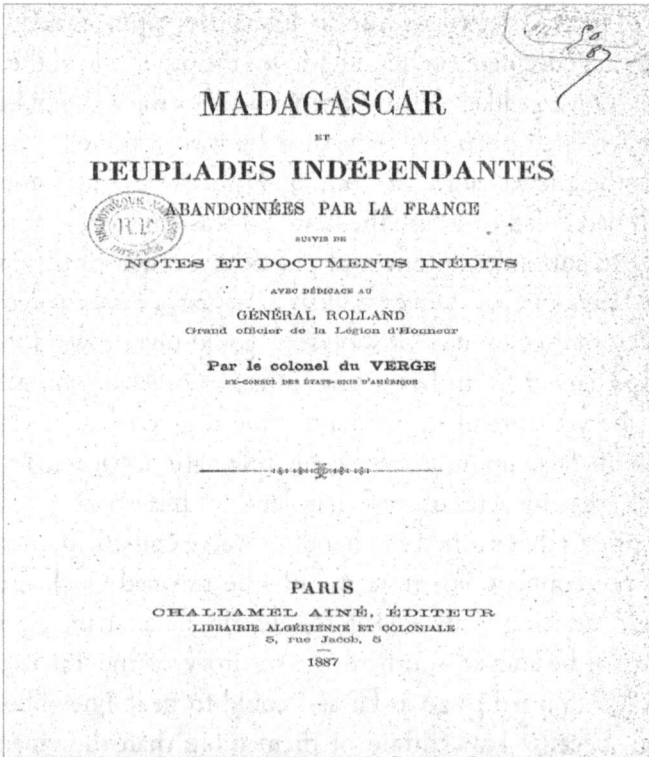

Cover, Duverge's Madagascar and Independent Peoples: Abandoned by France. *National Archives, Republic of France.*

Later, he would claim he sought help from an unknown writer to assist with some of the more difficult passages. Though Duverge felt incapable of capturing Madagascar's beauty, even with possible help, his attempts to document the customs of its people were successful. *Madagascar and Independent Peoples* records the governance of rural villages, the varying practices of religion in the island, and the agricultural practices of each region. Duverge regularly inserted himself into local ceremonies and religious customs, ingratiating himself with local leaders and tribesmen. Not having any authority to be cruel and needing to stay modest to remain safe, he was uncharacteristically cool-headed throughout these adventures.

And they were adventures.

Duverge claimed he had crossed Madagascar "with the first American flag that has ever been deployed in these regions, the most fertile soil in the whole world [that] had never before been trampled by the feet of any white man."[29] It was a perilous journey, and Duverge knew it. He described Madagascar as "the cemetery of Europeans" but pushed on anyway.[30] He explored the island with all the accompanying adventure and risk. While among the Tanalas, Duverge boasted to them that he was an accomplished soldier. Some of the warriors were skeptical and called for a demonstration. Duverge was instructed to kill a water ox standing five hundred yards away if he wished to remain a guest in their territory. The prospect of banishment, or worse, was present if he were to fail. "I dropped to one knee and secured my good, trusty rifle. However, it must be admitted, I had a certain little shudder at the thought that if I were to miss the cow I might be lost. I fired and my bullet struck, perhaps by good luck, just in the middle . . . Afterwards, the king and the chiefs were convinced that I had told the truth; they uttered atrocious cries, throwing their assaults in the air, struggling, jostling each other, and almost carried me in triumph on their shoulders."

Duverge then regaled his new friends with stories of life in Europe and combat in America. Before he moved on, the chief made him a blood brother, a ritual he underwent a half-dozen other times during his journey. Duverge seemed to hold a general affection for the rural population of Madagascar, who he viewed more positively than the Hovas. His writing implored French readers to view the Malagasy tribesmen as more than exotic primitives. He advocated for French intervention because of the potential he saw among Madagascar's various independent tribes. He even tried to claim a racial connection between some groups and Europeans. "The Sakalavians are people of a robust constitution and a pretty physique. Their color is much lighter than that of negroes, and with them they are considered to be true white men, as they are in fact, since almost all are the children or grandchildren of American whaling ships or Europeans having traded in this part of Madagascar."[31]

Duverge was wrong that "almost all" Sakalavians were the progeny of Europeans or Americans. This was not the only legend he reported as factual. In *Madagascar and Independent Peoples,* Duverge also included an account he recorded from the Ibara tribe of Madagascar's southwest. Clearly a parable, Duverge related it as true:

> [S]ome of them had once been in a canoe where there was only one slave to run it, with two oars. As the canoe only went very slowly and the slave could only use one paddle at a time, one of them suggested the idea of cutting the slave into two parts, and putting half of it in the front and the other half at the back of the canoe, to move the two paddles. This idea was immediately put into action. But unfortunately to their great displeasure and to their astonishment, they realized that cutting the slave in two had only resulted in killing him, and that the canoe, instead of going faster, was now stopped.[32]

As when he was in Angola, slavery was commonplace. Duverge reported that "coastal traders" abducted slaves from Madagascar's interior and took them to French-held ports, from where the victims were then sent to Reunion Island as "volunteers."[33] Unlike Loanda, where he had at least publicly objected to the slave trade, in Madagascar, Duverge was an admitted participant. Describing a chief who owned "two thousand slaves," Duverge claimed, "when I became his blood brother, he presented me with fifty young girls and boys."[34]

Less disturbing was Duverge's writing about the extraordinary wildlife of Madagascar and its importance to the local diet. He noted in detail how the various tribes hunted, committing no fewer than a half-dozen pages to the pursuit of sea turtles. He explained how the animals were captured ("the Sakalaves . . . make use of a stick approximately 4 yards long, made of a slender and strong wood. At its end is attached a small piece of iron about 4 to 5 inches long, carefully sharpened and the extremity of which is cut with a harpoon-shaped side") and then prepared for eating ("It is cooked with sea water and served in its own carapace.").[35] In Madagascar's interior southwest, Duverge encountered Mahafaly villages who used extraordinarily large eggs as pots. Duverge measured one of these containers and found it had the capacity to hold "no less than eighteen liters of water." Though he had not seen the animal, Duverge concluded that "a bird of formidable size" existed in the area.

Duverge's recitation of this event is remarkable for two reasons. First, the only bird capable of laying such a large egg was the so-called elephant bird (*Aepyornithidae*), which had been extinct since sometime around the thirteenth century. A handful of other European travelers to Madagascar in the nineteenth century reported rural tribes using apparent elephant bird eggs as pots, but documentation of this practice is limited. If Duverge's writing is accurate, it is a valuable contribution to the anthropological record.[36] Additionally, his report strengthens the credibility of the remainder of his account. His unwillingness to claim to have seen an extraordinary animal, unlike so many of his contemporary travelers from Europe who claimed to see everything in Africa, from unicorns to dragons, suggests that his writing was not entirely dishonest. Rather than capture the attention and support of his readers through mendacity, Duverge simply told the truth, easy as it would have been to embellish it.

But Duverge's expedition was not exclusively exploratory. His real mission was developing influence. While the book was ostensibly about the need for French intervention in Madagascar, his journey was as much about building his own political base on the island. The journeys in *Madagascar and Independent Peoples* record Duverge's attempts to establish relationships with key tribal leaders, men he could later use on a future expedition to the island, a visit for personal gain. And Duverge was fully prepared to do anything for it to succeed, including betrayal. Writing of the Hovas, his employers only a year before publication, Duverge called them subjugators of the island who were actually proxies for the English. He openly called for revolution against Queen Ranavalona, who, just a few months before, had granted him land in her dominion. Duverge claimed that the tribes not under Hova subjugation, especially the Sakalavas, among whom he had so deftly cultivated his own interests, would prefer to live under French rule—if only his French readers would appeal to their government to assist. When Duverge wrote of political matters, he departed from the mechanical style by which he described Madagascar's geography and wildlife. He instead adopted a more poetical, persuasive tone.

"The Sakalaves . . . were witnesses, during the last war, of the cowardice of the French who, after having driven them to rebellion, shamefully abandoned them to vengeance and to the cruelty of the Hovas. On the soil of Ibonia [a reference to a traditional Malagasy folktale] are many headless skeletons whose charred bones turn white under the fire of the sun, waiting to be avenged for such cruel murders and for such barbarous beheadings."[37]

During these passages, Duverge ceased to be an adventurer sharing amusing stories about strange wildlife and peculiar religious customs and, instead, wrote as an advocate, appealing to readers to alter existing French foreign policy. By that measure, Duverge's writing implicates him as a French agent far more than the rumors shared by Perraud. The structure and message of *Madagascar and Independent Peoples* is indeed similar to other works of French propaganda from this period, which typically appealed to the country's perceived moral obligation to expand its external influence, as well as the romance of foreign conquest. Duverge informed his readers that he wrote on behalf of fellow Frenchmen "who have suffered so much, so far from France, forgotten by their countrymen," and dedicated the work to his former Foreign Legion commander, Reunion-born General Charles Elie Rolland. Like Duverge, Rolland had fought as a legionnaire in Algeria and Italy (unlike Duverge, Rolland was an actual Legion of Honor winner). Duverge's editor, Augustin Challamel, was a French historian who published and edited dozens of popular works on historic and scientific matters during the second half of the nineteenth century, many of which advocated for increased French intervention abroad. Unlike Challamel's most popular writings, though, Duverge's book included no illustrations. Further, Duverge's "essay," as he labeled the two-hundred-page work, was published by the Librairie Algérienne et Colonial, a marque likely invented solely for this book. It seems less likely that *Madagascar and Independent Peoples* was a piece of official state-sponsored propaganda than it was a vanity project designed to promote Duverge's personal objectives in Madagascar, written entirely or mostly by the stated author.

While significant portions of the book are dedicated to attacking the Hova government and English missionaries, the strongest opponents of increased French influence on the island, Duverge also took swipes at personal enemies, including a certain U.S. consular agent. "The most illustrious Victor FW Stanwood, the consular agent of the United States, spends his days there in kingly fashion, stealing right and left, without any fear of punishment." In one passage, he praises German aspirations for African colonies, writing that he hopes Germany "will one day shake off the torpor in which it is plunged and will put aside the fear of the revenge of the French to focus its eyes on this beautiful island."[38] The prevalent theme in *Madagascar and Independent Peoples*, then, is not necessarily the importance of the French, but the importance of Duverge. The author presents himself as an essential interlocutor between the Sakalava people and other tribes in Madagascar opposed to Hova domination. This book was written for the benefit of Duverge and no one else. Duverge's true motive was to entice investment into his next scheme. Necessarily then, Duverge wrote positively of the island's potential, outlining its natural resources and commercial opportunities: "Europeans . . . with an amount of about 5,000 francs in canvas, old flintlock guns, powder, and mirrors and other articles of exchange could, by giving to kings and other chiefs, obtain a full concession to involve themselves and take away all the gold and other wealth they would like."[39]

France, it seemed to him, was the natural source of such foreign intervention: "Madagascar can today be conquered with five thousand men in the space of no time; but if France does not hasten to beat the iron while it is hot, it will take years, thousands of men and a lot of money to arrive at such a simple and beautiful conquest . . . Let France only give me a thousand well-armed good volunteers, I will take the whole country from [Queen Ranavalona III]."[40]

Corporal Perraud, who spent months with Duverge in the forests and plains of Madagascar, perhaps best captured the nature and hopes of the baron during this period. Perraud had initially viewed Duverge "as being a good man." He later revised his opinion, offering that Duverge "had a fiery, short-tempered, mean character. He was the embodiment of evil. However, he had a rare intelligence and was a great politician."[41]

This was a fair summation of Duverge at the time. He was immoral and irascible. But he was also clever in his relations with others. Duverge could use people effectively, if he could keep his pride and temper in check. A year and a half after abandoning his wife in New York, he returned to France and then America, intent on using his political acumen to fund his next plan.

CHAPTER FIVE

Death in Boston

D uverge spent most of 1886 in France. From there, he wrote a boastful letter to a friend in Baltimore about his Madagascar achievements. This friend, presumably with Duverge's encouragement, passed the letter to the local press, likely to boost Duverge's chances of identifying investors for his next scheme.[1] His next appearance in the American papers was not because of his adventures in Madagascar, past or future. It was because of the scandalous manner in which he met his second wife.

Duverge was always opaque when it came to marital relations. He likely lied to Reverend Thomas Gallaudet so that he could marry his first wife, Emily Simmons, before a famous minister. Duverge then misled Emily about his family and past life. He later sent her home from Angola to New York, promising to return but never doing so. In Madagascar, Duverge told Perraud various stories about his wife. He initially offered that they had met in Congo. Then, it was Louisiana. Later, he specified New Orleans. At different times, Duverge claimed she was living in America, Africa, or that she was dead. He showed Perraud a set of diamond earrings and told him that these belonged to his wife, but he gave no explanation as to why he was carrying her jewelry. The entire matter was a mystery to Perraud, who, despite acting as Duverge's confidant for over a year, never learned if the man was or was not married.[2]

While Duverge's first marriage was mysterious because he was not forthcoming, his second marriage was mysterious because of the violent, desperate nature of a different man.

The Marquis de la Tourasse was an impoverished French aristocrat who had escaped to Canada after accumulating significant debts in

Europe. He eventually settled in Boston, earning a meager living as a French tutor. He lived with a woman he claimed was his wife, though his first wife was still alive in France. He and the woman in Boston had a child together. In January 1887, she died while giving birth to a second daughter. "August de Sempe," an alias the Marquis had adopted to hide his past life, found himself desperate. Destitute and now with two young children, the Marquis contacted his first daughter, Marie Cailleres, in France and implored her to come to America. To do so, he lied to Marie. The Marquis told her that he lived a comfortable life and that she would be happy if she joined him in Boston. Marie, then just eighteen years old, believed his claims. She arrived in New York in April 1887 aboard the French steamer *Chateau Margaux*.

Marie was described as "refined and well educated" but "not handsome." Because her mother was also destitute, she had been living with moderately prosperous relatives in Toulouse. But her father's promise of luxury in America enticed her to adventure abroad. Upon meeting him in Boston, however, Marie realized she had been deceived. Her father, who insisted that she, too, adopt the name "de Sempe," lived in a modest two-bedroom apartment atop a four-story home full of lodgers. He was only barely surviving on his pay as a tutor. When the Marquis showed his daughter two children that he called her sisters and informed Marie that they would now be in her care, she was profoundly upset. The life of ease that her father had described to induce Marie across the Atlantic was a ruse. She resolved to leave America immediately. She told the Marquis she would briefly visit New York to see friends she had met onboard the *Chateau Margaux*. Then, she lied to her father, saying she would return to him in Boston. Her father was suspicious and tracked her down in New York. Somehow, he convinced her to return with him to Boston. Marie would later report that she followed the Marquis because she felt a sense of obligation to the man who was her father, even if he had abandoned her and the rest of his first family in France. Her return to Boston was brief, though. She was unhappy watching her young half-sisters and uncomfortable in the Marquis's spartan apartment. On May 20, Marie again decided to leave. She quietly purchased a train ticket to New York. When the Marquis discovered she was gone, he rushed half-dressed to the train station, leaving his two-year-old alone in the street. He arrived just as the train was leaving. The Marquis pushed past the conductor, shouting that he needed to speak urgently with his daughter, and charged from car to car in search of Marie. When he found her, the two quarreled. Marie made it clear she would not return. The Marquis threatened to kill her and then abruptly went silent. He walked to the door of the speeding train, opened it, and tossed himself onto the tracks—dying instantly.

The *Boston Globe* ran an extra edition that evening to cover the spectacular news of the disgraced French noble's suicide. "In Despair, Marquis de la Tourasse Ends His Life," shouted the headline, followed by details of how the "profligate nobleman" had been "inveigling his daughter into his clutches."[3] The next day, the front page again featured news of the Marquis's tragic end, promising readers more on the "Failure of His Deep Laid Plot and the Sad Sequel." By the third day, the story was nearly played out. There was a brief mention of "Marie in violent hysterics" that described a visit to the funeral home, but that short piece was relegated to the bottom of the page. All of the reporting to that point had ascribed the suicide to a dispute between father and daughter, a story that had limited long-term potential. But a correspondent in New York City soon uncovered another angle: the man from the steamship *Chateau Margaux*, a Captain Louis Duverge.

Marie's saga quickly became a headline again.

Duverge, "a fine appearing man fully of 45 years of age, of very dark complexion and commanding appearance," told the *Globe*'s New York reporter that he had met Marie during the April sailing of the *Chateau Margaux*. They became friendly because of their shared language and aristocratic heritage. The two parted ways when she traveled to Boston to begin her new life with her father, and he went to stay with friends in Jamaica Plain. But Duverge soon heard she was back in New York, where he called upon her. Marie explained her father's true condition and that she had decided to run away. Duverge advised her not to do so. The Marquis then appeared in New York and, finding his daughter with Duverge, confronted the seemingly wealthy captain about his intentions toward Marie. Duverge explained that the two were merely friends. He had taken an altruistic interest in Marie while they were at sea. After they arrived in America, he had given her his card in case she were ever again in New York. Duverge told the Marquis that she was safe with him. Nevertheless, Marie's father entreated her to return with him to Boston a second time. Duverge made a counteroffer. He would buy a house in New York. When he went on his next seafaring journey, the Marquis and Marie could watch the house for him. In fact, both Marie and her father could stay in his house, without cost, as long as they liked. While the prospect of free housing must have appealed to the impoverished Marquis, he rejected Duverge's proposal, presumably because it was absurd. Durvege was three decades older than Marie and, according to his account, had met her mere weeks before. The Marquis, likely sensing Duverge intended more than just charity toward his young daughter, ordered Marie back to Boston.

When the *Globe* reporter inquired if Duverge had ever proposed to Marie, he claimed he was already married. Duverge refused to share his wife's location other than to say she was outside of America. When pressed for more information, he replied, "She is not here; that is enough." Duverge then ordered the journalist not to publish any of his comments. The *Globe*'s editors ignored Durverge's request. The following day, the paper published an "Amended Version" that allowed Duverge to clarify his earlier statement. Duverge emphasized that the proposal for him to rent a home for use by Marie and her father had originated with the Marquis, not Duverge. Duverge also added that "he bears special decorations from the British, French, Italian, Belgian, and Turkish governments for special services in war and diplomacy."[4]

Having no decorations of his own and being now three days dead, the Marquis could make no rebuttal to Duverge's claims.

On May 24, "August de Sempe" was laid to rest in Canton, Massachusetts. His rest was to be temporary, though. Under the terms of the agreement with the undertaker, the Marquis's body was to be disinterred on June 26, taken from the casket, embalmed, and then placed in a different casket inside a metal box. Marie would then transport her father's remains to France via New York. Shortly after this initial interment, Marie secured a death certificate from a doctor that characterized the Marquis's final moments as an accident. Although several witnesses stated he deliberately jumped from the train, the death certificate determined that the decedent's wounds suggested he had fallen unintentionally. Such a finding was convenient for Marie. If the Marquis had committed suicide, it would have prevented his honorable burial in a Catholic cemetery. As it was, Marie sailed from France on July 13, three days before a Massachusetts inquest concluded that her father had indeed killed himself. She returned to France aboard the *Chateau Margaux*, certificate of accidental death in hand. Duverge was likely on the vessel, working (fortunately for him only temporarily; two years later, the *Chateau Margaux* would sink in the English Channel after colliding with another vessel).

Marie and Duverge traveled together as husband and wife. The two had married in France in March 1887, a month before their arrival in America. They had lied to the *Globe* and to her father about their relationship. Why they kept the marriage a secret is unknown. Maybe Duverge feared his first wife had never finalized their divorce. Perhaps it was their age difference. Maybe the two sought to determine how wealthy her father was in America before deciding how best to approach him for support. Regardless, their marriage might also have been the cause of the Marquis's seemingly spontaneous suicide. Perhaps as they were arguing on the train Marie had told her father she was returning to her secret husband, who was a mere three years' difference in age from the Marquis. Perhaps she even told him she was several months pregnant (she would give birth in October 1887).[5] In any event, the public soon lost interest. Despite famed *Globe* crime reporter Henry G. Tricket's claim that it was "The strangest case ever recorded in Boston," within a few months, the story was forgotten.[6]

Duverge and his pregnant teenage wife moved on as well. Immediately after burying Marie's father, Duverge returned to America and established himself in Boston. Much of what is known about his life from this period is derived from the notes of Perraud, who also found himself in Boston.

Perraud had left Madagascar aboard the schooner *Alice*, a journey marred by the presence onboard of "a filthy monkey who created a large amount of havoc."[7] His lot did not improve once he reached America. He barely spoke English, making it difficult to find steady employment. He found Boston unimpressive; Perraud was particularly disappointed to learn that the city's public establishments closed on Sundays. The fevers he had contracted in Madagascar persisted, and he spent most of his meager earnings on doctor and hospital bills. Life in America was hard. Perraud was delighted then, despite their earlier difficult relations in Madagascar, when he learned that Duverge was now in Boston. He discovered this from a *Globe* article titled "French Conversation." Curiously, Perraud's diary provides only selected information about that piece, which was actually a subtitle from the May 23 *Globe* interview with Duverge. Perraud limited his recollection of that article to the fact that Duverge had become involved with a young French noblewoman in New York and that he would soon arrive in Boston. He omitted all details of the Marquis's shocking death and Duverge's tangential involvement.

Instead, Perraud wrote about his reintroduction to Duverge. Near starving when he heard of Duverge's return to America, he visited the *Globe*'s offices to learn where his former acquaintance might be found. He then proceeded to Duverge's rented home on Asylum Avenue. Duverge was shocked at first when he saw Perraud, but then greeted him warmly and "served a good bottle of wine, which we did credit to." Duverge invited Perraud to join him on his next expedition to Madagascar, for which planning was already underway. Perraud declined Duverge's initial invitation to accompany him to Madagascar but agreed to dine with him again in the coming days. The two met several times after that, Duverge no doubt paying for dinner as Perraud was unemployed at the time. Duverge showed Perraud the *Solitaire*, the schooner he would eventually sail to Madagascar, and introduced him to some of the men he had recruited for the journey. He also introduced Perraud to millionaire William Emerson Baker, who offered Perraud employment at his hotel.

Perraud accepted.

Baker owned the Hotel Wellesley, a monstrous structure of three hundred rooms he had constructed in southwestern Massachusetts after accumulating a fortune in the sewing machine business. There, he dabbled in social advocacy related to the natural sciences, especially public health. To that end, he used his hotel and the attached gardens to promote his ideas about improved animal husbandry. Baker kept a menagerie of animals on the property for study and the entertainment of his guests. Perraud, who never shared precisely what he was hired to do at Baker's hotel, recorded "bears, buffalo, peacocks, peccaries, porcupines, monkeys, and turtles" present at the Hotel Wellesley. The hotel featured ninety stables, a massive ballroom, a shooting gallery, game rooms, and a restaurant. A regular schedule of expert speakers presented talks upon Baker's areas of interest. Perraud took particular note of the windmill that powered a series of fountains, and offered irrigation to the gardens and a large lake.[8] That lake was blemished by the presence of a sunken steamship, which had previously been used by hotel guests for pleasure cruising. To remedy that problem, Baker engaged Duverge to salvage the sunken boat. Duverge's experience as a mariner would have included extensive experience refloating ships that had become grounded. Extricating a pleasure boat from a Massachusetts lake would be an easy task for an experienced captain. He and Baker agreed that in exchange for removing the damaged vessel, Duverge would be allowed to keep the boat's steam engine. After several attempts, Duverge succeeded in removing the vessel from the lake at the end of the summer, receiving its engine as his payment. That engine, Perraud stated, was "destined for a boat that would be built in Madagascar to ascend the river."[9]

In addition to the engine, Duverge took Perraud back to Boston with him. Gradually, Duverge's offer of another Madagascar adventure became more appealing. While in Boston, Perraud signed onto the Madagascar expedition for $25 per month for one year. He was to work as Duverge's valet until sailing. His duties as a valet in America were much broader than those in Madagascar. One of his chief responsibilities was watching Duverge's mischievous teenage brother-in-law, Joseph Cailleres, who had come to join Marie and her adventurous new husband. Additionally, Perraud was in charge of Duverge's two prized French poodles, work he viewed as demeaning but temporary. Duverge assured him that once aboard, he would serve as a cook. A few weeks later, though, Duverge gave the cook position to another man, James Ridley Middleton.[10] Perraud protested. Duverge calmed him by promising work as the ship's carpenter. While loss of the cook's job reminded him of Duverge's duplicitous nature, Perraud had no other prospects. He accepted the new arrangement and set to work as a carpenter upon the *Solitaire*. His immediate task was to construct additional bunks to accommodate the ship's soon-to-be-hired crew. He was also tasked with expanding the vessel's hold, possibly with hidden compartments. Such preparations would be necessary for the vessel to surreptitiously transport the illicit arms Duverge intended to smuggle into Madagascar.

The *Solitaire* was originally owned by Arthur Sewall, who had ordered the schooner in 1879 when he was president of the Maine Central Railroad. Sewall later came to national attention in 1896 when he ran unsuccessfully for vice president alongside Democratic presidential candidate William Jennings Bryant. Duverge appears to have been vested with the captaincy of the vessel in 1887 by his wealthy friend Baker, who, at that time, was apparently the sole owner of the *Solitaire*. Duverge and Baker were likely partners. For several years, Duverge had boasted to anyone who would listen that his contacts along Madagascar's west coast were half of the formula to instant riches. All he needed to complete the scheme was investors. Apparently the dashing, decorated veteran of the recent Franco-Hova War had convinced the spontaneous, fantastical millionaire to invest in the possibility of gold mines in distant Africa. Unfortunately for Baker, Duverge had a plan to profit from the *Solitaire* even before she left port, and it involved taking advantage of his partner's generosity. As captain, Duverge was responsible for managing the ship's affairs. Baker would have expected Duverge to make needed improvements to the *Solitaire* and handle the vessel's accounts properly. But while Duverge set to work expanding the schooner's hold and adding bunks for a larger crew, he borrowed too much and paid back too late. The ship was seized by creditors. This malfeasance was part of Duverge's deliberate plan to force Baker out and to take sole control of the *Solitaire*. He had estimated correctly that when Baker learned of Duverge's poor accounting practices, he would sell his shares in frustration. Then, Duverge could quietly repurchase the *Solitaire* at a depressed price.

Perraud, learning of the plot, said to himself, "And this man was the former American consul!" and began to rethink his own future with Duverge. As he viewed it, "we were to be paid for going to Madagascar, a country that has no laws but where there surely would be trouble . . . I believed this man [Duverge] capable of doing anything . . . He will constantly lead me into trouble."[11] In October 1887, realizing Duverge was as dishonest as ever, Perraud left the *Solitaire*. Apparently Duverge's next dog sitter was less capable than Perraud. In December, Duverge placed a classified advertisement in the *Globe* offering a reward for the return of one of his French poodles that had gone missing. Perraud, meanwhile, moved to New York City, where he found work as a doorman at a large hotel. In later years, he married a Frenchwoman, relocated to California, and spent decades working around the world in the petroleum industry, dying in San Diego in December 1942.[12]

Duverge's plan to buy the *Solitaire* at a reduced price failed. Baker did sell. But not to Duverge. Either he was unable to find financing or other parties outbid him, because the successful bidder on the *Solitaire* was not Duverge but the Boston shipping firm of Dole and Flint. Fortunately for Duverge and his hopes of a return to Madagascar, the firm agreed to finance his expedition, although at a less generous amount than had Baker. No doubt his history of poor management of the vessel's affairs contributed to their reasoning. The firm also insisted on installing one of their representatives, B. Webb Dole, as a passenger on board the *Solitaire*. Dole would observe Duverge's work and maintain power of attorney over the ship and its cargo, which consisted of consumer goods to be sold at a moderate profit in Madagascar. Duverge would still have an interest in the expedition's profits, but at a reduced rate. Consequently Duverge's scheme, as so often his schemes did, backfired. He was in the same position he had been before he tricked Baker, but with less financial support and without title to the *Solitaire*. And he was being watched by B. Webb Dole.

In addition to the already engaged cook, Middleton, Duverge hired a cabin boy, Henry Gass. He then set about acquiring additional crew members. Duverge did so with the promise of treasure. He offered a share of his own profits from the expedition in exchange for lower wages. Duverge boasted that his relationships with native tribes, including his bonds of blood brotherhood with influential Sakalava chiefs, assured that the crew would have unchecked access to the immense mineral wealth of western Madagascar. It was similar to the spiel he had offered Baker, Dole, and Flint. Bostonians Charles Stebbins, William Simmons, James McDonnel, and B. F. Burbank accepted, joining the *Solitaire* for minimal pay but with the understanding that they would receive a cut of Duverge's profits from the adventure. An agreement to this effect was signed in Boston on February 14, 1888, binding the men to "Executive Officer" Duverge of the "Madagascar Trading and Development Company" for three years, in consideration for a share of the company's future mining proceeds.

Duverge's luring of Stebbins into his adventure was particularly sinister. Stebbins, a restaurateur by trade, had recently lost his savings to a business partner and was dangerously in debt. Duverge advanced money to Stebbins in exchange for a promissory note and a pledge to join the crew of the *Solitaire*. Stebbins accepted, seeing a way to discharge his debt and gain a new fortune in Madagascar. However, the note, written in French, entitled Duverge to not just repayment of the loan, but a claim against Stebbins' future inheritance. Stebbins was unaware of this until a native French reader reviewed the note for him and informed him of the bad deal.

Duverge had other devious plans for his newly recruited crew members.

While the four investors-sailors were necessary for the voyage to Madagascar (the *Solitaire* was 1,500 tons and 213 feet long), Duverge did not need them all once he was ashore. He could train his Sakalava allies to mine; they would work for cloth or black powder, not profits from the expedition. He only needed one or two loyal men to direct the natives. Duverge was incentivized then to force the financially invested crew members to desert once they had reached Africa. He would also benefit from B. Webb Dole's departure, if it could be arranged, particularly since Duverge was carrying an illicit load of gunpowder, revolvers, rifles, and cannons to Madagascar, unknown to Dole.[13] Once Dole and the other four Bostonians were forced out, Duverge could land in Madagascar, sell his illegal cargo, and commence gold mining with his Sakalava allies. A crew for the trip back to Boston in the future could be procured later. Between himself, his brother-in-law Joseph Cailleres, his cook, and his cabin boy, he had more than sufficient manpower to oversee foreign labor. That effort absolutely had to yield results for him, however. Forty-eight years old with a young daughter and pregnant wife, his professional opportunities were severely limited. If Duverge returned to Boston without substantial profits, he stood to lose his own investment in the expedition, some $2,500 in funds and labor (approximately $85,000 in 2025), but more importantly, his reputation. Without gold, there would not only be no riches, there would be no future expeditions. It was essential that this adventure succeed in one form or another. Finding gold was ideal. If that failed, his only hope was intrigue, specifically: sabotage.

Aware that western Madagascar was not under the direct control of any of the European powers or the Hovas, Duverge understood that a stranded vessel was subject to the norms of the local tribes. As he had recorded in his book, "According to their laws and customs, a ship that sinks . . . becomes their [the Sakalava tribes'] property."[14] If Duverge did not locate valuable minerals after a reasonable search period, he would ground the *Solitaire*, feign worry, and then appeal to the closest consul for an accounting of the loss before returning to America. Duverge would arrive with an insurance claim in hand to assuage his investors. His Boston partners would be satisfied, and his reputation would be intact. Meanwhile, his profit from both smuggling and his cut from the Sakalava looting of the *Solitaire* would await him back in Madagascar. Maybe, if the vessel survived the beaching, looting, and abandonment, he could find a way to refloat the *Solitaire* and finally make it his own.

The scam promised generous returns.

It was somewhat charted territory for Durvege. Like the original conspiracy aboard the *Spyhnx* decades earlier, the plan required scuttling a vessel to defraud its owners and then recovering the proceeds of the crime at a later date. A captain grounding a ship for personal profit was not unprecedented on the west coast of Madagascar. In 1886, an American barque had "stranded in fine weather" along Madagascar's west coast. The vessel's cargo then mysteriously disappeared. The captain of that ship demanded an indemnity from the U.S. consular agent in order to document the loss as a theft for insurance purposes.[15] That consular agent was Victor F. W. Stanwood, who granted the indemnity despite serious concerns about the legitimacy of the matter. Duverge knew, from when he first imagined his plot in Boston, that if he grounded the *Solitaire* in Madagascar, Stanwood would be dutybound to investigate. He calculated that if the *Solitaire* grounded in the same fashion as the *Surprise*, Stanwood would record the loss for authorities in Massachusetts as recoverable from insurers. Stanwood was an unknowing but essential participant in Duverge's potential fraud.

Grounding a ship had its dangers, but so did other aspects of Duverge's scam. Abusing crew members to the point of desertion risked a mutiny. Smuggling arms into lawless western Madagascar was also dangerous. And gold mining in the island's interior was hardly a safe

enterprise. Duverge was well aware that, eighteen months before his service under Willoughby, two American adventurers had been attacked by
several dozen natives armed with rifles and spears in Sakalava country
while searching for gold.[16] One of them, Charles Emerson, died from
his wounds. The two were accompanied by a French interpreter and several local guides but were nevertheless cut down by natives unwilling to
tolerate foreign prospectors. In that incident, as with the grounding of
the American barque later, Consular Agent Victor Stanwood managed
subsequent legal proceedings, making an appearance himself soon after
the deaths to conduct an investigation.[17] Stanwood, Duverge understood
then, was watching the west coast closely.

On February 16, 1888, Duverge and his new crew set sail for Madagascar. Aboard were Dole, Duverge's brother-in-law, his wife, and his
daughter, Louise, who had been born a year before in Shrewsbury, Massachusetts, and was sometimes called by her middle name, Henrietta.
Interested parties in Madagascar were aware of the group's impending
arrival. On March 24, the *Madagascar Times* in Antananarivo, the
island's largest English-language newspaper, published an attack on
Duverge. The piece claimed he had speared a servant (possibly a confla-
tion of Duverge and the Hova soldiers who had wounded Perraud) and
that, contrary to Duverge's claims after leaving the Hovas, during the
war he had had no qualms about killing French soldiers. He had also,
it was alleged, been expelled from the island. Someone in Antananarivo
evidently wanted to dampen French support for "Colonel Duverge"
before his return to the island.

Duverge, meanwhile, was trying to make the voyage as difficult as
he could for his crew members, in keeping with his plan. McDonnel
was the first to crack, becoming drunk one night and verbally attacking Duverge and the others, screaming, "you dirty black son-of-a bitch,
you damned Dutch son-of-a bitch, you damned French son-of-a bitch."
Duverge responded with discipline, the nature of which was unfortunately not recorded in the ship's log. After a stop in Sierra Leone for an
unknown period of time, the *Solitaire* arrived in St. Helena in April.
There, Duverge added three travelers, Daniel McDade and the Howe
brothers, David and Henry. McDade, an experienced American mariner,
contracted to do "prospecting, mining, sailing of schooner 'Solitaire' or

whatever office that said Capt. de R. du Verge may require from me" for six months in exchange for one-quarter shares of whatever he might find in prospecting. Duverge was obliged to provide McDade with food and, in the event he needed someone else to captain the vessel, wages of $75 per month. The Howes were Irish prospectors who had learned their craft in the goldfields of Australia. They originally joined the Solitaire as passengers destined for Natal, not as employees. But a month at sea with Duverge boasting about the riches of Madagascar enticed them to join his adventure. On May 29, the Howe brothers, joined by McDade, who amended his earlier agreement, signed a contract with Duverge, committing to three years of work in exchange for "one quarter share each of all kinds of minerals and precious stones found."[18] Duverge had now considerably diluted his own share of any potential profits. It was imperative that he find a way to drive away the crew members who had invested earlier.

Duverge's cruelty toward those men and Dole increased. He assigned harsh duties and handed out excessive punishment. By the time the Solitaire arrived in Africa, relations were severely strained. Duverge reacted by arresting five of the men on board, claiming a mutiny was imminent, alleging that "the crew generally since they left Boston have been in a mutinous state and always been insubordinate."[19] Four of these five, quite conveniently, were those who had joined him in Boston and expected to be paid in gold in Madagascar. The fifth was Dole. Duverge had all five put in irons and ordered the remaining men, who just happened to be the new sailors hired in St. Helena, armed.[20] The Solitaire then departed for Port Natal (present-day Durban). There, Duverge claimed he telegraphed the Solitaire's owners in Boston for more funds and a full power of attorney, arguing that the crew was unruly and that he needed more power to control the vessel and to make the expedition profitable. Duverge alleged they obliged, sending him £250 (approximately $45,000 in 2025) and the requested authority. It seems likely that Duverge lied about any correspondence with Dole and Flint in order to shore up his claim to authority with the Howes and McDade. It was imperative that the new men aboard believed he had full authority over the Solitaire and that his expedition was well supported and worthy of continued participation. The vessel's papers, though, recorded no change in power of attorney. At some point while in Natal, Duverge released his prisoners. He made peace with Stebbins, Simmons, and McDonnel—whom, just a few days before, he had beaten unconscious. All three agreed to continue on to Madagascar, likely viewing continued abuse as a better option than forfeiting their investments through desertion. Dole and Burbank had enough, however. They disembarked and located the American consul. Burbank asserted Duverge's conduct amounted to a breach of contract and that he was therefore not a deserter. Dole demanded the consul act to prevent Duverge from continuing the expedition so as to preserve what remained of Dole and Flint's investment. It was too late. The *Solitaire* was again at sea.

On July 6, 1888, the *Solitaire* reached Madagascar's west coast. Duverge anchored along a desolate beach, raised two American flags, and fired cannons. He told his crew that this was to summon his friendly contacts ashore. Simmons, now back in Duverge's good graces, joined the captain in a small boat. The two rowed ashore, "armed to the teeth." There, Duverge, dressed in the uniform of U.S. Army major, procured in Boston, met with a local chief and explained that he had been sent to Madagascar "by his big white king." The reception was cool, however, and Duverge returned to the *Solitaire* to seek out closer native friends. After several days of sailing back and forth along the coast, the vessel put in at Morondava, where it was greeted by the American consular agent, Victor Stanwood.

CHAPTER SIX

Stanwood of the West Coast

Victor F. W. Stanwood was born in Boston in either 1823 or 1824, where he claimed his family had lived for "as long as there was a Boston."[1] Stanwood's early adult life was spent at sea. In 1877, he visited Madagascar and, for seven months, explored the island's interior. Three years later, he settled near Morondava, one of the few places in Madagascar's southwest that was under some degree of Hova control and therefore relatively safe for the handful of foreigners who lived there. Stanwood was the only American. He led a lonely existence, apparently by choice. A woman in South Africa alleged to be married to Stanwood; he denied her claim. Another woman in Australia wrote to him about their child; he never responded. At one point in the 1880s, he told a visiting warship commander that he had a daughter who had attended Vassar and was married to an American naval officer. Stanwood spoke only rudimentary French but understood several Malagasy languages. He was said to be short with a dark beard, light-gray eyes, and large muscular arms that were elaborately tattooed.[2] Beyond this, nothing is known of Victor Stanwood's personal life or appearance.

The origin of Stanwood's service as a consular agent is also unclear. He lived in Andakabe, slightly inland from Morondava, where he made a living reselling goods from the vessels that sporadically stopped along the coast. Stanwood first appeared to the State Department in 1880, when he wrote and requested that he be made consul to "Mohabo, Madagascar." The department contacted Consul William Robinson in Tamatave to seek an opinion on the matter. Robinson agreed a new position was likely needed on the west coast, but he was uncertain if Stanwood was a suitable appointee. Robinson explained how, the year before, he had met a Norwegian captain who had visited Andakabe. There, the Norwegian encountered a man whom he characterized as a "humbug" and who claimed to be a U.S. consular officer. The impostor's name was "Stanwood." Robinson had dismissed the matter until he received the department's inquiry, whereupon he remembered the supposed consular officer in Andakabe. Robinson then learned that "Acting Vice-Consul" Stanwood was not only writing to the State Department, but the Hova government as well. Stanwood was demanding increased Hova protection against Sakalava tribes, claiming the natives had violated treaties he had negotiated. Such "treaties" (as well as the smuggling Robinson suspected Stanwood was facilitating) would have been a blatant breach of the Treaty of Commerce of 1867 between the United States and Madagascar, and a significant impediment to a revised treaty that the State Department was then pursuing. Fortunately for America's diplomatic interests, Robinson intercepted the fake consul's letters before they reached Antananarivo. He astutely noticed that one of the letters Stanwood posted to the capital from Morondava was mailed the same day he allegedly sent his letter from Mohabo to the State Department requesting a consular appointment. "How he could manage to write two letters on the same day—one from Morodava to [Antananarivo] and another to our State Department from Mohabo—two places 350 miles apart in a country, without railroads or other means of rapid conveyance, in fact where one is obliged to travel on foot, or be carried in a palanquinn [sic], which amounts to the same, relative to time—is a mystery!"[3]

Robinson also dismissed Stanwood's claim to the State Department that the best location along the west coast for a new consular agent was Mohabo. Rather, Robinson asserted, the only suitable location for a west coast presence was in Mojanga (present-day Mahajanga). Mojanga was the country's second-largest port and the only location from which travelers from Antananarivo could depart the country in the west. A long-established trading center, the town was populated by several thousand inhabitants, a "mixture of Sakalavas and Arab and Indian traders; with a Hova governor and a strong Hova military post." Mohabo, on the other hand, Robinson knew only as a small village located several hundred miles south of Mojanga. He dismissed locations distant from Mojanga as ungoverned and too dangerous: "The Hovas have established, from time to time, since their nominal conquest of the Sakalava country, a few, small, isolated military posts in the interior of the country; but not one on the coast from Mojanga south."[4] Robinson did concede that Stanwood's claim of a need for a consular presence in the southwest was potentially warranted, noting: "what he says in regard to trade and the need of a consular officer on that part of the coast may be partially correct, or perhaps wholly so."[5] Robinson estimated that the potential for trade in the region was significant and that a consular agent there could facilitate legal and proper growth of commerce. Additionally, he hoped that a State Department officer could clarify the ambiguity that surrounded the July 24, 1879, visit of the USS *Ticonderoga* to Andakabe.

The *Ticonderoga* was the first U.S. Navy steamship to circumnavigate the world, and the first American warship to visit Madagascar's southwest in thirteen years.[6] In addition to showing the flag in distant ports, the *Ticonderoga*'s commander, Commodore Robert Shufeldt, carried broad instructions from President Hayes to expand American trade where possible. Shufeldt, a former U.S. consul to Havana, negotiated agreements with foreign governments from Africa to Asia, gaining significant concessions in Korea in particular. While in Madagascar, Shufeldt had achieved an agreement from the Sakalava tribes to permit American vessels to trade in areas they controlled. This grant meant American merchants could evade the 10% customs fee the Hova government imposed on imported goods. Rumors of this "treaty," never seen much less ratified by the authorities in Antananarivo, frustrated Robinson, who was working to negotiate better relations with the Hovas. Robinson documented his complaints by sending the State Department a list of the problems created by the commodore's meddling, which ranged from empowering anti-Hova tribes in the southwest to inaccurate reports about instability within the Hova government.[7] His opinion was that Shufeldt's treaties should be "thrown into the wastebasket."[8] Given all of this, Robinson doubted Stanwood was the right man to serve as consular agent. He informed the State Department that he suspected Stanwood was involved in a "clandestine trade," but of a relatively benign fashion wherein he imported goods to the parts of the west coast that were not under Hova control in order to avoid customs dues.[9] Nevertheless, the State Department instructed Robinson to contact Stanwood and determine his suitability for a position as a consular agent. Robinson did so, writing to Stanwood and asking a list of questions about the region's economic potential and governance. He made no mention of Stanwood's alleged improprieties.

This non-confrontational approach was typical for Robinson. While Stanwood was repeatedly described as "direct" and "loud" by those who met him, Robinson's nature was cautious and passive. This was despite his significant military service during the Mexican-American and Civil Wars, which included action as a Union officer at Second Bull Run, Chancellorsville, Gettysburg, and Cold Harbor. Robinson was a capable advocate for U.S. positions, but at this point in his life, he preferred to fight through letter-writing. He rarely left Tamatave except for regular holidays in Reunion. He was most comfortable in his office or at representational events, accompanied by his secretary, an Oxford graduate and sometimes journalist for the *Madagascar Times*.[10] The Hovas indulged Robinson's affinity for pomp, welcoming him on his first visit to Queen Ranavalona II's palace with two days of feasts and gifts of livestock. Inside the palace, which Robinson believed to be twice the size of the White House, he observed that "the general appearance of the state-room reminded one of the English or French courts of the 16th century, perhaps a mixture of the two for they have evidently copied from both."[11] In a series of meetings with the queen's officials, Robinson renegotiated key parts of the 1867 Treaty of Commerce, including a provision that would allow consuls to try American citizens in Madagascar for crimes committed against other Americans.[12]

Stanwood, meanwhile, was in austere Andakabe, where he was in receipt of a State Department letter that related some of Robinson's claims, including the assertion that Stanwood was engaged in illegal trade. He was furious. He could not understand why Robinson was asking him about commerce on the west coast while simultaneously informing the State Department that he was dishonest. Direct as always, Stanwood wrote to Robinson, "I am immeasurably astonished at this information."[13] He then explained that the confusion about his use of a consular title was justified. When the *Ticonderoga* had arrived in

Andakabe, Stanwood had appeared and offered assistance. As one of only a handful of Americans living along the southwest coast, Shufeldt adopted Stanwood as a representative of his mission. Unbeknownst to Robinson or the State Department, Shufeldt had conferred the title of "acting vice-consul" upon Stanwood so that he would carry more gravitas during the commander's negotiations with local tribes. Therefore, Stanwood explained to Robinson, he had every reason to believe that he was indeed the acting vice-consul for the region. He had written to Washington to clarify the situation.

Learning this, Robinson softened. He even admitted that he might have been wrong earlier. Perhaps Stanwood had not lied about his location when he mailed letters to Antananarvio and Washington. Robinson had since learned that there were actually two "Mohabos." The Mohabo he knew was distant from Andakabe, but the other was much closer to where Stanwood had supposedly written. Possibly his earlier implication that Stanwood was dishonest was incorrect. Robinson did note, however, that Mohabo was still a three-day journey from Andakabe.[14] He pursued that anomaly no further, though. Receiving reports that Stanwood was devious but also "energetic and driving and . . . doing much good at that point in pioneering foreign trade," he dropped all objections to his appointment.[15] Their détente culminated in November 1881, when Robinson communicated to Washington:[16]

> Not being acquainted with Mr. Stanwood, and having knowledge of
> the crooked ways many men follow in this country, taken together
> with his deception in assuming to be Consular officer, thinking that
> the act was wholly self-suggested for objects of vanity, or worse, I
> formed an opinion of the man which was probably to some extent
> erroneous. . . . I am inclined to think that he would make an excellent
> consular officer for that particular district. Therefore I nominate
> Victor F.W. Stanwood of Boston, Mass., for consular agent at Anda-
> kabe, for the district of Menabe, and ask that the proper outfit for a
> sea-port agency be sent out.[17]

Robinson had surrendered. While Stanwood was likely engaged in smuggling, he was, if nothing else, at least American. And if he assumed consular duties for the miserable southwest, then Robinson would never need to visit there. Stanwood was formally appointed the following October, but it took until December 1882 for him to receive "the proper outfit for a sea-port agency" (which consisted of some office supplies and a consular seal).[18] Initially, Stanwood's service was quiet, although he did register complaints about commerce and instability in the region. He grumbled that Europeans dominated trade and lamented that there was not "a large American house on this coast, independent of Mussulman interests or any foreign influence whatever, which would take a little pains to find out what articles were worth handling, and push them."[19] Stanwood also noted the continued practice of slaving. One of his first public reports was quoted by the Foreign Office in London, which had no representative in western Madagascar at the time. After explaining that Stanwood had observed one hundred slaves being exported from his district, the foreign minister reported to Parliament that: "From these few but authentic recent incidences, it is evident that, although the Slave Trade may be dying out, it is dying hard; but with three cruizers in these waters, and the splendid establishments of the London's boats, with the now loyal aid of the Sultan of Zanzibar, and the awakened activity of the Portuguese, I hope next year to report a very great decline."[20]

The optimism was excessive, as Stanwood would soon record.

Following the conclusion of the First Franco-Hova War in 1886, Stanwood increased the volume of his reports to Washington. No longer was he documenting routine trade or sending receipts requesting reimbursement of official expenses. Stanwood commenced a comprehensive campaign of letter writing designed to draw attention to what he saw as a dramatic increase in the slave trade along the island's west coast.

Madagascar had prohibited the export of slaves in the early nineteenth century. A robust domestic slave trade, upon which much of the island's social and economic structures were balanced, continued unabated until its eventual ban in 1896. But by 1865, European naval vessels, and occasionally American warships, enforced bans on slaving in the region with limited success. While the Atlantic trade all but ceased in the 1860s with the ending of slavery in America and the prohibition on the importation of slaves into Brazil, other major routes persisted. Arab slavers continued to bring slaves from Madagascar to the Persian Gulf region. Indian traders did the same, but to the subcontinent. Both groups used Madagascar as a transit point for slaves captured on the African mainland (Stanwood estimated up to five thousand souls were trafficked in this manner in 1884).[21] Additionally, creoles from French-possession Reunion and British-controlled Mauritius transported Africans to work on island plantations in what was, at best, a form of oppressive and indefensible peonage. Aside from the domestic trade within Madagascar up until 1896, all of these activities were illegal. But Hova control of the island was nominal outside of their centers of power, and where it existed, corruption was endemic. Antananarivo held only two ports on the western side of Madagascar in 1886, and there only weakly. Further, the 1869 opening of the Suez Canal had shifted shipping routes to the north of Madagascar, which meant the naval powers that professedly policed the high seas moved north as well, making the west coast more appealing for slavers. In addition to the slave trade expanding, the smuggling of arms in the region had increased during Stanwood's tenure, raising instability.[22] Stanwood documented his observation of these developments around Andakabe and the danger to himself, writing in August 1887 that: "The slave dealing commenced to increase in 1884, continued to do so through 1885, and at last in 1886 an Englishman commenced it here in the very face of the governor and exportation was also carried out on at the south, on a large scale, and now that there is no control here those slavers will most probably attempt to kill me or burn my house, or both. I have been attacked more than once in former years."[23]

Stanwood believed that the British consul in Tamatave, W. Clayton Pickersgill, was ignoring or even complicit in this smuggling. He even claimed that Pickersgill was knowingly issuing passports to slave traders from India and other British colonies. Stanwood was also angry about how foreign vessels would fly the American flag "as a kind of insurance policy."[24] This practice occurred because there was a widely held perception that an American ship could not be searched. In a legal sense, this was not correct. Madagascar's navy was incapable of policing its waters, possessing only a single steamer and "pirogues and canoes."[25] But European powers had the authority to search American vessels suspected of slaving or other illegal activities.[26] In a practical sense, though, America was no longer a viable market for slave traders, so ships flying the

Stars and Stripes often avoided scrutiny. What patrols still existed in the Mozambique Channel focused on vessels other than those from the United States. Further, unlike the European states that had pretensions to Madagascar, America was viewed as a neutral country best left unmolested. Vessels from the United States were not known for smuggling arms or delivering missionaries with their troubling political ambitions, as were European-flagged ships. Malagasy authorities and native tribes were inclined to view Americans as less threatening than other outsiders. As such, the American flag was often flown by non-Americans, at sea and onshore. Stanwood documented these abuses in a series of missives he sent directly to Washington, claiming that communication with the consulate in Tamatave was unreliable.[27] As long as the U.S. flag could be flown by anyone and smuggling continued unchecked, American opportunities for trade in Madagascar were hindered, Stanwood argued. Emphasizing that regular visits from the U.S. Navy to the southwest had been promised but not materialized, Stanwood opined, "it had become evident that the effort to promote foreign commerce is to be confined to printers [sic] ink."[28]

Why Stanwood became so consumed with drawing official attention to the slave trade is debatable. The handful of modern assessments that exist have characterized him as an unburnished champion of liberty, fighting gallantly against the evils of slavery. The State Department press release adding his name to the department's memorial wall in 1931 stated that Stanwood "had been active in endeavoring to stop the slave trade on the west coast of Madagascar."[29] *Overtime in Heaven*, a compendium of stories from the Foreign Service published in 1964 by journalists Peter Lisagor and Marguerite Higgins, devoted an entire chapter to the narrative that Stanwood was a noble soldier in the battle against slavery.[30] That portion of the work is a highly fictionalized account of Stanwood's efforts to raise attention to disorder on the west coast. Lisagor and Higgins culled the consular despatches from Madagascar to select quotes that presented Stanwood as passionately fighting against the evil trade and then decorated those reports with their own conclusions. They made no mention of Stanwood's potentially disreputable past or possible smuggling. Inventing a more acceptable motivation for his complaints, the authors offered solely that "the immorality of the slave trading was in itself offensive to the devout consular agent at Andakabe."[31]

But Stanwood's contemporaries held him in a much less illustrious light. Campbell, who was deeply religious and abhorred slavery, described Stanwood as engaged in "clandestine trade." Duverge had mentioned Stanwood as "stealing left and right." Following his death, two different Australian women claimed to be his wife, making it possible that Stanwood had been married to two or even three women simultaneously. Bigamy was likely not his only offense in Australia. An 1879 warrant in New South Wales sought Stanwood for criminal conversion. Authorities advised that Stanwood, believed to be English (an impression others had of Stanwood, too, despite his claims to be from Boston), had sold boats in Adelaide and Wellington to which he did not hold title. Stanwood then escaped to Madagascar, the warrant expiring without his arrest.

EXTRACTS FROM VICTORIA POLICE GAZETTE

[From Police Gazette, 5th November, 1879.]

MISSING FRIENDS.

Information is requested of Benjamin Webster Hands, formerly in the Mounted Police, Victoria, and subsequently groom at the "Horse and Jockey Hotel," Wangaratta, he was afterwards employed as a striker in a blacksmith's shop, Lachlan River, N.S.W. The last that can be ascertained of him is about a year ago, when he was stockriding on the Ballondryin Station, N.S.W., kept by Mr. Rankin. His whereabouts is required in consequence of property having been left him.—O.6381. 4th November, 1879.

Information is requested of Robert Westwood, of Bolton, Lancashire, England, a rag merchant, who emigrated to Melbourne in the year 1857 or 1858. His wife and daughter followed him a year afterwards. A letter was received from him in 1860, in which he stated that he was carrying on business as a herbalist or herb doctor in Melbourne. It was asserted about 3 years ago that Westwood was not living with his wife, and that he allowed her maintenance, and that his daughter was married to a wealthy man in the colony.—O.6262. 4th November, 1879.

MISCELLANEOUS INFORMATION.

The whereabouts is particularly required of a man named Victor Francis Warren Stanwood, who was formerly second mate of the ship "Lucy Turner," trading on the African coast, and subsequently was captain of the schooner "Madeline," which vessel he sold at Adelaide about 1877. In September, 1878, he was captain of the barque "Courier," and unlawfully sold the same at Wellington, New Zealand. Description of Stanwood :—About 40 or 45 years of age, 5 feet 2 inches high, iron-gray hair, dark beard, whiskers, and moustache, light-gray eyes, very round shoulders, large muscular arms which are elaborately tatooed, very loud voice, a native of the Isle of Wight ; and was last heard of at Maryborough about November, 1878. He is believed still to be in one of the colonies. Warrant issued. The above offender must not be arrested, but information of his whereabouts forwarded to Detective Office, Melbourne.—O.6352. 3rd November, 1879.

Stanwood wanted by Australian Police, 1879. New South Wales Gazette.

While there is no evidence Stanwood ever condoned slavery, his surge of interest in the phenomenon happened to correlate with his financial well-being. As the largest American trader in the southwest, Stanwood held an important position in the region. He imported and resold goods and doled out tribute as needed to promote his business. He was a man of influence. But following the war, there was a spike in the prices of slaves and a change in the regional market.[32] Suddenly, the economy, in which Stanwood had finally started to scratch out a living, shifted rapidly—likely to his detriment. Illegal slaving generated more revenue for local chiefs than Stanwood's minor trading enterprise, and concurrently, his economic influence over local officials diminished. Additionally, the importation of arms that accompanied the trade of slaves would have damaged local stability and Stanwood's potential to sell goods. It is possible, then, that he suddenly cared so much about slavery because it was costing him money. In addition to economic changes, the surge in slaving brought unwelcome political changes to the American consul. His close contact and protector Governor Rakota, a Hova appointee to the region around Andakabe, was suddenly removed—allegedly under pressure from slavers. The new governor, Stanwood claimed, attempted to collect excessive customs duties in contravention of the American-Malagasy Treaty of Commerce. He reported, "trade utterly at a standstill, the new duties levied by the Malagasy government having driven everyone except myself and one more into the Sakalava districts."[33] Without Rakota to guard him, Stanwood's new world was not only less lucrative, it was more dangerous. Particularly if Stanwood himself had been dealing in illegal goods. And especially if he objected publicly to the practices of the slave traders—which he did.

Stanwood wrote to anyone who would listen about the perils of the west coast, particularly the southwest where he resided. He wrote to Antananarivo, complaining about the removal of Rakota. He wrote to Washington about the increase in slaving. He wrote to the French resident about English missionaries, who he supposed were ignoring the slavers deliberately. He even wrote to the British consulate, accusing London of quietly enabling illegality ("Will your foreign office **do** anything?").[34] And he wrote to the U.S. Consul in Tamatave about everything.

Whether Stanwood's motivation arose from moral objections to slavery or from selfishness about the loss of business, his voluminous writings were largely ignored. During his final two years on the island, Consul Robinson failed to respond to Stanwood's despatches. At one point in 1886, Stanwood became so desperate for information from the U.S. Consulate in Tamatave that he again wrote to his nemesis, British Consul Pickersgill, this time asking for assistance with Robinson instead of chastising the English for enabling the slave trade. Pickersgill could offer no help, though; Robinson had already resigned his office. He was replaced by John P. Campbell in February 1887. Campbell arrived in Madagascar carrying autographed photographs of President Grover Cleveland and First Lady Frances Cleveland, twenty-seven years the president's junior and the subject of international attention so intense it had even spread so far as Antananarivo. The photographs were a gift for Queen Ranavalona III, who had succeeded her aunt, Ranavalona II, in 1883. Her Majesty reciprocated by giving the new American consul six chickens, four geese, a goat, and an ox.[35] After Consul Campbell distributed his gifts and received his animals, he returned to Tamatave. There, he inquired of his vice-consul, R. M. Whitney, about the peculiar man sending letters to the American consulate via the British. Whitney responded:

> Concerning Mr. Stanwood, I consider him thoroughly unreliable, and
> my opinion is based on what I know of him through official corre-
> spondence when I have had charge of the consulate, and on what I
> have heard of him from many sources including businessmen who
> have had correspondence and transactions with him, and through our
> Naval officers. He is known at Mauritius, Capetown, Natal, and Zan-
> zibar and from none of these points nothing favourable I have ever
> heard about him and to some of them he appears to be considered
> an adventurer. I know Boston and New York houses that have had
> dealings with him that now would not have one cent of their money
> get into his hands.[36]

Based on that ringing endorsement, Campbell took his time responding to Stanwood, adding the continued messages from Andakabe to the large stack of despatches already assembled in the consulate. He did so despite Stanwood's increasingly spirited criticisms of inaction from the United States government. Stanwood wrote directly to the

State Department, demanding an American ambassador be appointed to Antananarivo and that he be made a full consular officer. He was ready, he informed the department, to commence negotiation of a new treaty with the Hovas himself. Stanwood objected to the haphazard manner in which the American military dealt with local officials, a complaint well-known to professional diplomats then and now. He blamed U.S. naval vessels for negotiating with local tribes and undermining Hova authority, asking: "Will U.S. Naval officers <u>never</u> learn how this country stands in relation to the United States?"[37] Receiving nothing from Washington or Tamatave, he unilaterally decided to convene a consular court to adjudicate a dispute about a vessel between its two owners, a proceeding for which he had no authority. The judgment was later successfully appealed on the grounds that a consular agent was incompetent to hold such a proceeding. Eventually, Stanwood captured Campbell's attention. The *Madagascar Times* published a February 1888 piece accusing Stanwood of a conspiracy with his friend Governor Rakota, who was then under arrest for corruption. Stanwood attributed Rakota's arrest to slave traders who resented the man's integrity. Stanwood also impugned the British community on the west coast, including the English missionaries there who he claimed cared more about weakening French Catholic influence then ending the slave trade, Consul Pickersgill included. But as the *Madagascar Times* saw the matter, "Mr. Stanwood has for years been in mysterious connection with the late governor in some very auspicious dealings with the Sakalavas. So much so that the property of the town was entirely ruined, the Sakalavas having fled the place because they alleged they were blackmailed by the governor, and Mr. Stanwood."[38] Stanwood was furious, describing the article to Campbell in a letter he wrote:

> To speak of it as an outrage is to give it too mild a characterization. It is infamous. It is a clear denial of natural rights and, as such, is utterly indefensible. By going into the service of their country men do not forfeit a surrender of those rights which are the indispensable safeguards of honor. I believe that the Secretary of State will promptly insist upon an investigation that shall show up the whole business when the facts are brought to his knowledge.[39]

Stanwood's threat to tell the State Department that he was personally in jeopardy was enough to earn a letter from Campbell, the first communication between the consulate and Andakabe in more than two years. The new consul finally addressed Stanwood and his increasingly clamorous correspondence in June 1887. He informed the consular agent that Robinson had left the consulate in a state of disarray. Campbell assured Stanwood that communication from Tamatave would now be more regular. And he promised to forward Stanwood's many earlier messages to Washington.

He did. In July, Campbell sent the State Department a massive package of unanswered despatches and personal letters from Stanwood to Robinson. He informed Washington that he was sending "Complaints from U.S. Consular Agent Stanwood of the sad state of disorder existing on the West Coast. With protest to this consulate against the threats of two British subjects upon his life. Up to the present I have refrained from sending a special despatch to the Department upon this subject, as I have to be very prudent and somewhat guarded as to Mr. Stanwoods [sic] statements, for I am informed he has a reputation for exaggeration"[40]

Campbell had other concerns. The French resident in Antananarivo was engaged in a dispute with the Hova government about the nature of his authorities. When Campbell attempted to receive diplomatic accreditation from the resident, Prime Minister Rainilaiarivony reacted by ordering the French resident expelled, arguing that the treaty between the Hovas and the French did not include authority for the resident to accept foreign diplomats on behalf of Madagascar. The French briefly lowered the flag of their mission and threatened to leave, taking with them the investment and support that had flowed into the island since the peace agreement had been reached two years before. The matter was quietly settled, though, and Consul Campbell was encouraged by Washington to avoid any further acts that might inflame either the French or the Hovas.[41] It is understandable then that Campbell might have been focused more on matters in Tamatave and in Antananarivo than in Madagascar's west coast. He barely had the energy to respond to Stanwood's endless wave of complaints, let alone take note that Duverge had returned to the island.

Murder in Belo

Though Campbell probably had no notice of Duverge's arrival, Stanwood likely did. Most of Stanwood's unanswered communications were official despatches, but he had also transmitted several personal, unofficial letters to Tamatave. A message sent in early 1887 specifically concerned gold mining. Stanwood had learned that American prospectors were working deposits in the southwest. He added that he was pursuing a concession but admitted he was not certain where or how to begin getting approval, given the chaotic nature of authorities in the region. Stanwood also shared he was aware of another expedition being planned from Boston.[1] It is quite possible this was Duverge's new "Madagascar Trading and Development Company." When Campbell eventually responded to Stanwood, he encouraged support for any potential American prospecting expeditions: "I do not see why we should not render them all the assistance we could and not only that give them all the information at our command."[2]

Perhaps because of that instruction or because of his own initiative, when the *Solitaire* appeared in Morondava in mid-July 1888, Stanwood was there for its arrival. Duverge, who had attacked Stanwood publicly in his book, asked the consular agent to let "bygones be bygones." Stanwood agreed. He invited Duverge to dinner, where relations warmed further. Soon the two were discussing shared business interests.[3] Duverge had men, equipment, and connections with Sakalavas. But he lacked rapport with authorities in Morondava, which Stanwood possessed. Such contacts would be valuable if the enterprise ever reached the level both men believed was possible. The two former enemies saw potential in their mutual interests and formed a partnership, hidden from the crew of the *Solitaire*. From July 25 until August 3, Stanwood sailed aboard the *Solitaire* as the expedition explored the southwest coast, going as far south as Nosy Ve, or Sandy Island, a small island just offshore from the Onilahy River delta in Madagascar's southwest.[4] McDade and the Howes were set ashore at the mouth of the Mangoky River, one of the longest waterways in Madagascar. Duverge claimed to hold a concession to ply the Mangoky in a steamer, a then worthless grant considering the steam engine he had rescued from Baker's lake remained in Massachusetts.

Nevertheless, the three men were instructed to make their way inland, locate Duverge's Sakalava allies, and commence prospecting. Duverge gave the men "3 Spencer rifles, 60 Spencer rifle cartridges, 3 revolvers, 150 revolver cartridges, and 600 yards of cloth." The *Solitaire* then put in at Belo, where a tidal harbor permitted relatively easy inspection of the ship's hull. Duverge wanted to examine the *Solitaire* for "shipworms," tiny mollusks that affix themselves to wooden ships and then gradually bore into the hull and rudder. Shipworms could degrade the structural integrity of a hull, potentially leading to catastrophic failure of the entire vessel. His decision to visit Belo was prudent, given the *Solitaire* had been at sea for several months.

After that stop, Duverge returned to Nosy Ve, disembarking Stanwood in Morondava along the way. While in Nosy Ve, most of the men decided to leave the expedition. Duverge wrote to Stanwood on September 4, complaining that the crew had been induced to leave by a local English trading house "who wish to crush our competition."[5] Duverge refused to pay the men's salaries, considering them deserters. He noted that without a full crew, he would be forced to return to Morondava, having aboard only his cook, cabin boy, wife, and "servant" (his brother-in-law, Joseph Cailleres), as well as "a few natives" he had hired. Notably, he asked Stanwood to assess the potential damages if the ship should be lost while "deprived of the men he needed to explore his potential claims." It seemed Duverge was ready at that moment to run the vessel aground. But before sabotage was necessary, the disenchanted crew returned to the *Solitaire* and Duverge sailed to Morondava. Once there, he encountered more bad news. McDade and the Howes had abandoned mining and were now working their way to Stanwood. When they located him, they claimed they could no longer serve under their abusive captain. The men asked Stanwood, under his authority as a consular agent, to release them from their contracts and absolve them of any claims of desertion. The other crew members soon renewed their calls to leave the expedition.

They likely were not quitting because of Duverge's harshness. His oppressive style of leadership was nothing new to the crew. What was probably more troubling was the realization that his promise of easy wealth in Madagascar was illusory. He had assured his crew that his friendship with important Sakalava chiefs—his blood brothers, no less—would unlock the island's treasures. All the Madagascar Trading and Development Company men needed was to find their way to Madagascar and the gold would appear. The problem, though, was that the concessions Duverge received from Sakalava chiefs during his journey across Madagascar in 1885 were, three years later, mostly forgotten. While it appeared he still had some association with the tribes along the shore, Duverge no longer held significant influence among the Sakalavas in the interior, where support was most needed for gold mining. According to a later review of his operations, "there is not a paper in existence granting to Captain du Verge any lands or mines in the South West part of Madagascar nor has he taken any steps looking to the occupancy of mines."[6] After several weeks of sailing up and down the coast, it was obvious to his crew that Duverge had no special access to undiscovered gold deposits. Duverge's promises had been so exaggerated that his men wondered if there had ever been a plan to search for gold. Consul Campbell believed it so, writing later:

> The large number of persons on board so small a schooner is accounted for from the fact, that several of them were . . . to locate and work gold, copper, or any other mines, that are said to abound on this island. That the intention of the Master and part of the crew was to conduct mining operations is I am satisfied evident. Such operations however, were to be in South West Madagascar in the territory occupied by and belonging to the Sakalava.

And the Sakalavas of the interior, as the *Solitaire*'s crew discovered, were not desirous of another gold-prospecting expedition. Duverge's boastfulness, bolstered by his book and Hova war decorations, had been persuasive in Massachusetts. But in southwest Madagascar, his claims were quickly shown to be exaggerations. His men found themselves on the opposite side of the globe from their homes, led by a malicious captain who had taken their money and labor and introduced them to a dangerous and unprofitable place. They were ready to do anything to get away, and enlisted Stanwood for help.

While the evidence was overwhelming that the captain had been abusive of his crew and misleading about the prospects of their expedition, Stanwood's sympathies initially rested with Duverge. He wrote to Campbell to give his thoughts on the dispute. Stanwood noted that the vessel's logbook indicated that the crew had been "turbulent and insubordinate" since departing Boston and that more than once they had "threatened to scuttle or burn the vessel." He believed that the men were exaggerating Duverge's conduct so as to appeal to the U.S. government for a claim of "subsistence and transportation," as well as an escape from their duty to the expedition. The consular agent had passed a week on board the *Solitaire* and had recorded no complaints at that time. Their unwillingness to work was actively encouraged by English traders in Madagascar, suspected Stanwood. These were the same traders he believed were trafficking slaves. In Nosy Ve, the English had actively tried to entice the crew of the *Solitaire* to leave, using drink and promises of work. In addition to cruelty, McDade and the Howes accused Duverge of smuggling. They signed declarations before Stanwood that the captain had landed powder and firearms at Morondava, a charge Stanwood at first dismissed. Perhaps because he understood that if the crew actually left, the expedition was finished. The *Solitaire* was a "unique American vessel," and it required an American, not local, crew. If Duverge attempted to sail it alone, the ship might very well be lost. In Stanwood's opinion, the future of the Madagascar Trading and Development Company was in a perilous state. Naturally, Stanwood's quiet business relationship with Duverge might have influenced his willingness to overlook the complaints of the ship's crew and side with the captain.

Despite the risk of losing the *Solitaire* if he sailed with only his skeleton crew, Duverge chanced a quick passage to Mozambique the next week. There, he cabled his financiers in Boston for more support. With his men threatening to flee and his expedition faltering, an infusion of funding was perhaps his only hope. The effort failed. No doubt Dole, who had been abandoned in South Africa two months before, had already communicated to Boston that Duverge's captaincy was a disaster. With no other choice remaining, Duverge pointed the *Solitaire* east toward Madagascar, ready to execute his plan of last resort.

On October 1, 1888, Duverge intentionally grounded the *Solitaire* at the entrance to Belo harbor. He was hoping his new alliance with Stanwood remained intact, that the consular agent would characterize the loss as insurable, and that he could preserve his reputation and future prospects in America through the loss of his own ship. As part of that scheme, it was necessary for him to play the part of dutiful captain. Duverge would later claim that English traders had paid a local pilot to drive him and his vessel into the sand. That claim would be central to his argument before the insurance brokers in Boston. But at the moment, he needed to demonstrate that he was acting to save the *Solitaire*. So Duverge sprung into action, evincing all the sincerity of a committed shipmaster.

He attempted to back the vessel away, only digging it in farther. Then, he engaged natives to remove the ship's cargo as he and his small crew jettisoned ballast. He worked for days to right the *Solitaire*, seemingly frustrated with his bad luck. Stanwood soon arrived, angry former crew members in tow. While Stanwood had been sympathetic to Duverge when he had first returned to Madagascar, seeing the *Solitaire* upon the beach reversed his sentiments entirely. He was convinced that Duverge had acted deliberately and, in doing so, thwarted their own business relationship. Duverge denied this. He implored Stanwood to order the crew back to assist the *Solitaire*. Stanwood denied the request and, in fact, started to assemble statements to not just release the men from Duverge's expedition, but to seize control of the *Solitaire* from the captain. He returned to Andakabe to prepare the necessary papers and communicate the affair to the consulate in Tamatave. Over the next few weeks, he would move back and forth between Andakabe and Belo, some twenty-five miles, documenting the plight of the *Solitaire*.

Duverge continued to go through the motions of attempting to right the vessel. In a drastic move he claimed was necessary to save the

Solitaire before she became permanently stuck on the beach, he had her masts cut and removed. Finally, on October 18, the *Solitaire* was moved into a small bight where the vessel was afloat at high tide and aground at low tide. The shipworms continued their insidious feasting upon the *Solitiare*'s hull, slowly eroding the bottom of the ship that had already been butchered atop.[7] Duverge's former crew members, several of them investors, watched this disassembly of the *Solitaire* in horror. They knew that as the ship became less and less salvageable, their own losses approached totality. The men also understood that their former captain had the motivation to do so, suspecting he had arranged with the local Sakalavas to sell the vessel's illegal cargo for a profit. And they were certain Duverge had grounded the ship intentionally. McDade and the Howes informed Stanwood that after arriving in Madagascar and finding the expedition's future less than bright, Duverge had told them he would sail to Mozambique to implore his Boston investors for more support. If that failed, "he would run said schooner *Solitaire* on shore at Andalanda [near Belo], would abandon her to the natives and when that was done, his blood brother, a certain Sakalava chief, known as Ramananga, would return said vessel to him as owner, and that the rightful owners would be left without remedy."

Learning this, Stanwood was now fully convinced he needed to protect the *Solitaire* on behalf of Dole, Flint, and any other investors. Duverge challenged him, but Stanwood insisted that the name of the Boston firm on the ship's paper was the owner, not Duverge. He issued an order under his authority as consular agent instructing Duverge to cease any contact with the remains of the *Solitaire*. Belo being one of the few ports in the area under Hova control, Stanwood mustered guards from the customs house to secure the wreck against further Sakalava looting or visits from Duverge. He then dutifully inventoried what remained of the vessel's cargo. Stanwood ordered the Hova guards to secure "75 ½ kegs of powder and 29 rifles, three bayonets, 7 rifles from Belo, 4 cannon with apparel, 1 box of bayonets, 2 box of revolvers and cartridges." Plainly, the expedition was about more than ordinary trade. Also listed were "two snow shovels" and an American flag (given Stanwood's complaints about abuses of the Stars and Stripes and the local climate, the flag was likely more appealing to would-be looters than the snow shovels).[8]

On October 13, Stanwood wrote to Campbell that he was relocating indefinitely to Belo. He submitted that his regular attention to the *Solitaire* was necessary, or else the affair would result in a disaster similar to the plundering of the *Surprise* three years earlier. Despite the Hova guard, the *Solitaire* was being picked apart and "severe losses have occurred."[9] Concurrently, Stanwood finalized the process of dismissing the crew. Stebbins and Simmons were granted an injunction as representatives of "certain capital invested in the expedition," enjoining Duverge from incurring any additional expenses upon the credit of the *Solitaire*.[10] The same day, Duverge wrote Stanwood, requesting that he be allowed to send repairmen to fix the ship, advising that "our enterprise here was and is not an unlawful one, and that I shall try to the last of my breath to carry it through the best I know of." He knew that if the ship was left to deteriorate completely, his hopes of later reclaiming it from the Sakalavas would be lost. Duverge pleaded with Stanwood that "private feelings or business must be put aside, and real true and friendly help must be had not only for the owners and insurers of all concerned, and I call on you as an old shipmaster to have the Solitaire inspected." But the statement from members of his crew that Duverge had intended to strand the *Solitaire*, likely made during a characteristically self-destructive rant, was damning. There was no chance now that Stanwood would grant Duverge a document testifying that the ship's loss was insured. Paradoxically, for someone who had intended to ground the *Solitaire* and then recover its looted remains much later, Duverge now needed to quickly again get her afloat before the vessel was a total, unrecoverable loss.

Stanwood responded the next day, informing Duverge that his decision was final. Further, Stanwood issued a consular court decision eliminating any connection Duverge had to the wreck because "from the inception of the voyage he exhibited incompetency and mismanagement in the conduct of said enterprise, and such mismanagement did continue and become accentuated as the voyage did continue" to the point that he had lost any authority to act as captain. Duverge's former crew told Stanwood that Duverge had illegally given certain papers and cargo from the *Solitaire* to a French acquaintance in Belo; Stanwood demanded these be returned. Stanwood also ordered Duverge to pass to him the personal effects of crewmember Burbank, who had escaped the *Solitaire* in Natal in June. Stanwood informed Duverge that he did not consider Burbank a deserter because of the captain's excessive abuse and that he was therefore discharging Burbank of any liability. This would entitle Burbank to pursue Duverge later for his unpaid salary from the expedition. Stanwood also demanded that Duverge send him an accounting of wages due for Simmons, Stebbins, and cabin boy Henry Gass. The Howes and McDade were also suing Duverge via a consular court action, seeking $450 in unpaid wages. At the conclusion of this legal assault upon Duverge, Stanwood added a note that he was available to mediate between the captain and his now former crew.

Realizing he had completely lost Stanwood at this point, Duverge decided to appeal to the consular agent's superior in Tamatave. On October 28, Duverge wrote Campbell, "I have here now all kinds of trouble raised and caused by discontented young men: but above all by your subordinate, Mr. Stanwood, whose acts etc. now are merely with intent to spoil a good and honorable business, just at its infancy for the simple reason that he is one of my worst of enemies [sic]." Duverge informed Campbell that the vessel was only insured to Madagascar, not for losses after it was grounded. Since the ship had by then been moved off the beach, any further deterioration was not recoverable. Duverge requested Campbell remedy Stanwood's error in not declaring the ship a loss while it was still at sea. In exchange for such paperwork, Duverge offered to give Campbell the $2,000 he had staked in the expedition, writing, "take the whole place I have in the vessel and enterprise, but please come and give me and us all justice." Campbell considered the offer tantamount to a bribe and did not respond. Stanwood continued with his demands of Duverge. Most of the crew had now settled in Belo, where Stanwood had set up his presence in a one-man tent. He received complaints and filed judgments there as the crew and Hova guards monitored Duverge, who had taken residency in the home of a Frenchman. Middleton, the cook, had remained in Duverge's good graces until now. But influenced by the other crew members, he went to Stanwood and confessed that several weeks before the grounding of the *Solitaire*, he and Duverge had offloaded cargo in Belo. This no doubt reinforced Stanwood's suspicions that Duverge had allies near Belo and that the beaching of the *Solitaire* had not been by accident. It also suggested an urgency to resolve the matter, since Duverge's coastal Sakalava friends had an interest in the vessel, as had others. Meanwhile, the *Madagascar Times*, always several days distant from the news in the southwest, had finally learned of Duverge's arrival. Two months after the stranding of the *Solitaire*, the paper reported the following:

> It is some time since we heard of that renowned gentleman MR. VICTOR STANWOOD, the United States Consular Agent on the west coast of Madagascar. We hear that he has now joined forces with that other adventurer, Capt Du Verge, whose card bears the very heavy load of titles Brevt. Major, FRGS; C.M.B.G.S; U.S.V.V.U.S.C.S Captain Du Verge is once more among us, and with Mr. Stanwood some eggs are being hatched just now which are likely to bring forth interesting chickens.[11]

The *Madagascar Times* had detected that Stanwood and Duverge had decided to work together. It had not yet, however, learned that by early October they had fallen out. Information from the southwest only reached Antananarivo by messenger, either overland or via vessels that traveled to Tamatave or Majanga. Consequently, news was often stale or inaccurate by the time it arrived in the capital. Even the Hova government was poorly informed about this part of the island. Stanwood and the consuls in Tamatave regularly complained that Hova authorities would open diplomatic despatches before they reached their destination, not so much to spy on the Americans but merely to learn what was happening in the southwest.

On November 5, Stanwood wrote to Duverge about some property belonging to Simmons, Stebbins, and Dole that could not be located on the wreck. Stanwood instructed Duverge to return the items to him immediately "to prevent further possible trouble."[12] Duverge responded by advising Stanwood that the scraping of the ship (the removal of shipworms and barnacles from its hull) he had ordered earlier was complete. Lacking authority to do anything further with the vessel, he begged Stanwood to allow him to hire men to secure the exterior with protective copper paint. Stanwood informed Duverge that Dole and Flint were the owners of the *Solitaire* and he had no authority to order such improvements. Duverge now was completely removed from any control over his former vessel. All he could do was watch her deteriorate upon the beach.

There was not much to the town of Belo. Through some fate of tides and currents, the otherwise sandy coastline was interrupted by a small spit of sandy land that provided a modest port between Morondava and points south. There was barely a harbor, and what was there was un-dredged and shallow. Fishermen in dhows tended nets onshore and a handful of small structures, abandoned by traders and missionaries who had long since left and passed the properties on to locals or less successful adventurers, stood shabbily near the beach. The Hovas maintained a customs house in one of these dilapidated structures. Beyond the town was Sakalava country. At night the Hovas retreated to their feeble garrison, surrendering all but the town's center to their tribal enemies.

Duverge, his now visibly pregnant wife, their daughter, and his brother-in-law had moved into the house of Jean Baptiste Pargas, a French trader who lived along the beach immediately next to where the *Solitaire* was stranded. The structure was a single-story wooden home with a patio on the front side that faced the small bay. Two wooden fences surrounded Pargas's property. The exterior fence was slightly higher than a man. The interior fence was smaller, only rising to one's waist. Stanwood was situated a five-minute walk away, where he had erected his small tent and was studiously documenting matters related to the *Solitaire*. The customs house was to the north of Pargas's house, between Stanwood and Duverge's temporary residences.

A waxing crescent moon hung over Belo on November 5, giving little light to the few people who remained awake after dark. Madame Duverge put her child to bed. She then attended to her brother, Joseph, who was also inside the house. Outside, Duverge was sitting at a table conversing with the very drunk Pargas when the carpenter Encasse appeared. Stanwood, Encasse had been told, had a newspaper that said Duverge had been expelled from the island by the Hovas years before. Encasse, who was due money for the work Duverge had ordered, demanded to know if this was true. Duverge insisted it was not and challenged Encasse to produce the article. The carpenter visited Stanwood's tent. There, he found both the newspaper and former crew member William Simmons.

Simmons, who had been drinking, insisted on bringing the article to
Duverge. Simmons marched into the yard where Pargas and Duverge
were seated and accused his former captain of lying about the expedition's prospects from the beginning. Duverge denied this, as well as any
expulsion from Madagascar. He snatched the article and read silently
while Simmons, joined now by former crew member Charles Stebbins,
stood behind him, making faces and insulting noises. After finishing,
Duverge announced that the article included nothing about him being
expelled, which was very likely true. It seems near certain that the piece
in question was the March 8 *Madagascar Times* piece that accused
Duverge of condoning the killing of French prisoners. That article made
no mention of any expulsion from the island. But Simmons disagreed.
He declared that Duverge was a "fraud and swindler," to which Duverge
responded, "Will you stand up before me six feet with revolvers and tell
me that?" Simmons answered, "No, I will not stand before you six feet
with revolvers, but I'll stand before you with my fists."

Duverge spit in Simmons's face. Simmons, wearing metal knuckles,
struck him in the eye, knocking Duverge to the sandy ground. Duverge
collected himself and stood. The two grappled. Simmons fell on top of
Duverge. At this moment Marie Duverge exited the house with Joseph.
Both were carrying revolvers. Marie shouted to her husband, "Louis!
Louis!" and threw her revolver on the ground near Duverge.

Duverge would later assert that the weapon accidentally discharged
after being tossed to him by his wife. This seems unlikely, considering
the softness of the ground. Stebbins and Simmons were certain Joseph
had fired. Middleton, who by all accounts was sober, probably gave the
most accurate account. He saw Madame Duverge fire and *then* throw the
weapon to Duverge.

No matter how it happened, the crack of the pistol was enough to
break up the fight. Duverge stood and asked, "Who fired that shot?" Middleton informed him, "Your wife did." While Duverge tried to sort out
if someone had been trying to help or hurt him, Stebbins picked up the
revolver and ran out of the yard, Encasse and Simmons following. Joseph
chased after Simmons, but the larger man knocked him down, only to
release the boy after he pleaded for mercy. Duverge's wife, meanwhile,
implored her husband to go inside and dress his wound. At the start of

their fight, Duverge had not realized Simmons was armed with metal knuckles. The initial strike to Duverge's head rendered serious damage. Dvuerge's right eye was entirely swollen shut and bleeding profusely. By his testimony, it would take two months until he could see normally again from the wounded eye. Duverge stumbled into Pargas's house to find water to wash away the blood. When his wife attempted to light a lantern, he told her to extinguish it for fear of mosquitoes, reminding her that the baby was sleeping just a few feet away.

By now, Stebbins and the others had returned to Stanwood's tent. The consular agent demanded to know who had fired the round he heard. Simmons said Joseph Cailleres, Duverge's brother-in-law, had fired the shot at him after he had skirmished with his former captain. Stanwood announced that he had heard enough. He was going to arrest Cailleres. McDade agreed to join. Middleton pleaded with both men not to go. Stanwood allegedly said to him, "tis my duty, I must go." Middleton then handed Stanwood what he later claimed was a revolver without its chamber. When advised to wait for the other part of the weapon, Stanwood declared he did not need a loaded gun, only the appearance of one. After asking Middleton to go to the Hova customs house and tell the guards they were needed, Stanwood and McDade set out on the short walk to Duverge.

Three Hovas were already waiting when McDade and Stanwood arrived at Pargas's home. They remained outside the fence with Middleton while the two Americans entered, passing through both gates before stopping at the foot of the patio stairs. A faint light flickered from inside the house.

Stanwood announced, "Who's been doing this shooting?"

Duverge's outline appeared at the open door, looked down at the two men, and stated, "I've not been doing any shooting."

Stanwood, spotting Joseph behind Duverge, declared, "This is the boy who has been doing the shooting." He then ordered the captain of the Hovas to arrest Joseph. The captain did not respond. Stanwood determined he would do so himself. He stepped onto the veranda and put his hand on the boy's shoulder, declaring, "I will hold you as a prisoner and investigate the matter tomorrow morning."

A shot was fired.

Stanwood fell backward into the arms of McDade. Middleton rushed to assist as the Hovas fled around the side of the house. Another shot exploded, a different caliber, it seemed. Middleton and McDade hastily dragged the now silent Stanwood out into the street. In that rush, the men nearly snapped one of Stanwood's fingers when it caught on the exterior fence. They pulled his body through tiny Belo toward the consular agent's tent. There, they placed him on a mat. McDade tore open the victim's blood-soaked shirt, revealing a massive hole to the left of Stanwood's heart. He was dead.

Meanwhile, the sound of sporadic gunfire from Pargas's house continued, disrupting the quiet rhythm of the waves. The shooting carried on through the night as Duverge, terrified that his former crew was coming to kill him, maintained a wounded guard over the house, firing at any sound or motion he detected outside the fence. At sunrise, the gunfire ceased. A source from the village had informed Duverge that the other crew members were gathered around Stanwood's tent, uncertain what to do next. They displayed no willingness to attack. Duverge, too, was in no mood to fight. He had passed the night continuously shooting and reloading, a fact he would later deny. In addition to attending to his wounded eye, he had helped Marie sustain the gravely injured Joseph. The second shot that evening, the one fired after the round that killed Stanwood, had struck the boy in the abdomen. He had fallen down the house's stairs into the front yard before stumbling to the side of the structure and re-entering through a side door. There, Joseph's sister attempted to stop the bleeding while Duverge shouted orders and fought back against the shadows and sounds outside. Though exhausted and hurting, that morning Duverge and his family slipped away from Belo.

Simmons also fled. A week later, he appeared in Nosy Ve, where he then escaped to Boston, never to be seen again in Madagascar. But before sailing, Simmons told his story to others, who shared the information with the French consul. The French informed Consul Campbell in Tamatave, who learned of the tragedy on December 18. On December 21, Campbell sent a cable to Washington from Tamatave via Aden: "Consular agent Stanwood shot dead at Belo South of Andakabe November Fifth by Captain Du Verge of Schooner Solitaire."[13] The cable was an immediate notification of the news to Washington. A weighty diplomatic pouch, meanwhile, was being dispatched from Tamatave with a letter from Campbell and six enclosures that provided background on the tragedy. Campbell included what he knew of the assumed killer: "He claims to be an American citizen, and the report is current here that he once held a position in the U.S. Consular service somewhere on the southwest coast of Africa, but he by birth is a native of Mauritius."[14] It would take a month for that information to reach the State Department.

During that time, Campbell implored the Hova government to adhere to its treaty obligations and to capture Duverge. Duverge, meanwhile, played the victim. He sent a letter to the Malagasy minister of foreign affairs requesting assistance. Duverge claimed to be writing from Ampasiria, a settlement hundreds of miles inland from his actual position along the coast. This was certainly an attempt to hide his true location from the Hovas while still trying to gain their favor.[15] He also wrote directly to the American Consul and again offered a bribe if Campbell would only come to Tamatave and see for himself what had transpired. Duverge insisted that McDade had shot Joseph and that the consul was needed to assure justice was achieved. A similar note was dispatched to the local Hova governor. McDade, too, wrote Campbell for help from the United States government, begging, "We are seven Americans here in distress awaiting an investigation by Man-of-War or otherwise."[16] On December 14, the French resident offered Campbell the use of a warship to locate Duverge. The French official emphasized, "It is impossible for the Malagasy government to arrest Duverge, they lack the means."[17] Nevertheless, the next day, Campbell attempted once more to get the Hovas to assist. He emphasized the gravity of the charges against Duverge, the "offense not being even bailable." Campbell further asked for the accused and witnesses to be brought to Tamatave for a preliminary examination while he awaited "instructions from the USA about a trial."

But Duverge by then was ensconced in an old fortification, possibly a position he had engineered during the war. There, protected by his weapons and coastal Sakalava friends, he rested safely "in defiance of the Hova authority."[18] But it was a miserable existence. Still blind in one eye from his wound and Joseph half dead from his grievous injury, Duverge and his two-year-old daughter watched as Marie gave birth to a son from their place of hiding. Living off the land and food brought secretly from

Belo by natives, the small group struggled and starved along the coast, unsure of what to do next. The newborn soon died. Marie recorded that they wrapped the body in "plants and woods of this country" in the hope that the remains might one day be deposited in her family tomb in faraway Bordeaux.[19]

Back in Tamatave, instructions finally arrived from Washington. In February, the State Department advised Campbell that the sloop-of-war USS *Swatara* had been ordered to Madagascar to investigate the shooting, arrest Duverge, and convey him and witnesses of the crime to Tamatave. Campbell requested that the ship report to him first for instructions.

The commander of the *Swatara* disagreed.

CHAPTER EIGHT

The Trial of Duverge

Captain John McGowan Jr. started his career as a volunteer in the Union Navy. Initially a second mate, he earned successively higher positions, eventually achieving command of his own vessel. After the fall of the Confederacy, McGowan was commissioned into the regular navy. Much of his service was spent conducting operations outside of the United States. In 1887, he took command of the USS *Swatara*, a three-masted vessel that could be propelled by either wind or coal. The *Swatara* was assigned to the South Atlantic Squadron. In 1889, she was visiting Montevideo when McGowan received instructions to travel to China via the Cape of Good Hope. As McGowan's crew prepared for the voyage, their captain received amended instructions from the navy. The *Swatara* would now stop in Madagascar on its way to Asia.

The new orders derived from Washington's interest in the circumstances surrounding Consular Agent Stanwood's death. In the days after learning of the killing, the House of Representatives passed a resolution requesting more information about the tragedy. On March 1, 1889, the president transmitted to Congress "a report from the Secretary of State touching affairs in Madagascar." Secretary of State Bayard's findings amounted to thirty-three pages, mostly enclosures from the packet Consul Campbell had sent soon after he learned of the shooting. Bayard informed the House that the report constituted "all the information received by the Department up to the present time in regard to the killing of Mr. Stanwood, consular agent of the United States at Andakabe."[1] But they sought more information, and it would take a warship to find it. Additionally, Stanwood's presumed killer needed to be brought to justice.

As the *Swatara* sailed to Madagascar, Duverge and his family remained in hiding outside Belo. In April, he sent a message to Campbell, describing his family's hardship: "The misery in which we are now bodily and mentally I cannot find words to express, but it seems that it is like a drowned man crying for help which does not come." Duverge added that they were on the "starvation track." He wrote that McDade had shot both he and Joseph Cailleres. Duverge implored Campbell to visit Belo, not just to assist his family, but to preserve the *Solitaire*, which was "daily getting more and more spoiled." Still harboring some hope for saving his disastrous expedition, Duverge told Campbell he had a plan to place the island of Europa, an uninhabited atoll in the Mozambique Straits, "under the American Flag by act of congress 'for guano [sic] Island.'"[2] Duverge was referencing the Guano Islands Act, an 1856 statute that granted private citizens the right to claim *terra nullius* under the authority of the United States government if such locations were suitable for phosphate extraction.

Campbell did not respond to Duverge's letter.

On May 26, the *Swatara* arrived in Morondava. The ship fired a salute to the Hova governor, who soon informed McGowan that his men were unable to locate Duverge. Three days later, however, Duverge appeared and surrendered himself, his wife, his daughter, and his brother-in-law to the Hovas, who immediately passed the group to the *Swatara*. McGowan also accepted the boarding of Daniel McDade, cabin boy Harry Gass, cook James Middleton, and four Hovas as passengers, their presence as witnesses being necessary for eventual proceedings in Tamatave.[3] Before sailing, McGowan "had the body of the late Victor Stanwood exhumed and a medical examination made by Assistant Surgeon Field, U.S.N. with the view of determining how many shots had struck Mr. Stanwood and their character." At the request of Duverge, McGowan instructed a French-speaking officer to take the testimony of Jean Baptise Pargas, who refused to travel to Tamatave.[4]

On June 1, the *Swatara* set sail for Tamatave via Mozambique and the Comoros. During the passage, Commander McGowan spoke with Duverge, who "conceded that the first shot was fired by Mrs. du Verge" and that there was "evidence to show one of the two shots that entered Stanwood were from Cailleres." With that conversation, Duverge placed the blame for the shooting on his wife and brother-in-law, a claim he would never repeat. McGowan and Duverge no doubt also discussed their shared service during the Civil War, including time in Charleston. Duverge likely would not have mentioned the true circumstances of his jailing there. Instead, he would have played to McGowan's sympathies, lamenting that a devious consular agent had undone his attempts to promote healthy commerce between the United States and Madagascar. Duverge, an accomplished braggart and sycophant, would have exploited this time with McGowan to earn his support.

On June 15, the American warship entered Tamatave harbor and fired a twenty-one-gun salute in the direction of the Hova flag. The Hovas returned a courtesy salvo. Vice-Consul Whitney, who was managing the consulate while Consul Campbell was in Antananarivo, paid a visit to the *Swatara*. He was greeted by a volley of five guns, as was the custom. Whitney informed McGowan that only Campbell could formally accept the commander's investigation into the accused. However, Whitney would take custody of Duverge, although he was unsure where to maintain him or to what extent he should use consulate resources to support the others. This not being a problem for the navy, the commander disembarked the prisoner and witnesses and then approached the Hova government for permission to conduct target practice offshore. Permission granted, the *Swatara* commenced firing into Tamatave Bay, subjecting the people of the city to a final barrage after a day full of diplomatic cannon fire. Whitney, meanwhile, established an ad hoc jail next to his residence. He rented the adjoining house and moved Duverge and his family inside, placing a Hova guard in front of the building. Then, using consulate funds, he purchased food and secured lodging for the witnesses. Campbell returned two days later, exhausted from strenuous travel. He had been in the capital for several reasons: to negotiate a new treaty, to request that Queen Ranavalona III send men to secure the southwest coast, and to admonish Hova officials who had opened official messages between him and the late Stanwood. Once back in Tamatave, Campbell summarized his Antananarivo meetings in a message for Washington. He included in that despatch the handful of donations made by Malagasy citizens to victims of the Johnstown Flood tragedy, which had occurred two weeks before in Pennsylvania. Campbell then turned his attention to the 230-man American warship in the harbor, where McGowan was waiting to give his report before a soon-to-be-convened consular court.

Consular courts were tribunals established by a state in the territory of another country to adjudicate legal matters between their citizens. Descended from the early consular tradition that had emerged in ancient Egypt, nineteenth-century consular courts served mariners, travelers, and other citizens who were abroad and encountered a need to litigate an issue before a court of their own government. The authority for American consular courts emanated from Article 2, Section 2, which grants the president the power to make treaties with the advice and consent of the Senate, provided two-thirds of the Senate concur. Once the Senate ratifies a treaty, it carries the force of U.S. law. During the late nineteenth and early twentieth centuries, the United States concluded treaties with Morocco, Egypt, Japan, Turkey, China, Madagascar, and other countries that included provisions for consular courts. Such courts were usually established in states geographically distant from America which maintained systems of jurisprudence perceived as biased against U.S citizens. Legal systems outside the Christian tradition were of particular concern. As the Supreme Court noted in an 1891 decision:

> The intense hostility of the people of Moslem faith to all other sects, and particularly to Christians, affected all their intercourse and all proceedings had in their tribunals. Even the rules of evidence adopted by them placed those of different faith on unequal grounds in any controversy with them. For this cause, and by reason of the barbarous and cruel punishments inflicted in those countries, and the frequent use of torture to enforce confession from parties accused, it was a matter of deep interest to Christian governments of withdraw the trial of their subjects, when charged with the commission of a public offense, from the arbitrary and despotic action of the local officials. Treaties conferring such jurisdiction upon these consuls were essential to the peaceful residence of Christians within those countries and the successful prosecution of commerce with their people.[5]

Madagascar, on the far side of Africa and with a collection of faiths and traditions alien to nearly all Americans, seemed a suitable location for a U.S. consular court. Accordingly, such authority was included in the 1867 treaty between Washington and Antananarivo. In the two decades between then and Stanwood's death, U.S. consuls in Tamatave had regularly issued consular court decisions for minor commercial disputes. Stanwood himself had convened consular courts in Andakabe. Under this authority, for example, he had determined members of the *Solitaire* crew could be dismissed from their obligations to Duverge. But a homicide trial was a much more serious affair. Consul Campbell was not an attorney, but like all consuls, he was expected to be versed in the law. He had some help. His local interpreter understood several languages and was an excellent notetaker. Vice-Consul Whitney could aid in procedural matters, as well as attending to any regular consular business during a potential trial. And as a law library, Campbell had an assortment of law books his predecessor had ordered from the State Department in 1879.[6] These men and texts were the instruments he would use to establish and run a consular court to try Duverge.

He would have preferred not to.

Campbell had hoped the *Swatara* would take Duverge back to the United States or remove the accused to another American diplomatic legation. Captain McGowan, however, only had orders to locate, investigate, and transport Duverge to Tamatave. After that was achieved, his instructions were to continue his voyage to China. With Duverge in his charge, and lacking any guidance from Washington, Campbell decided to proceed with a local trial. But he had no jurors. Duverge had a Sixth Amendment right to an impartial jury composed of his fellow citizens. But only two Americans resided in Tamatave and one, Consul Campbell, was serving as judge. The other, Vice-Consul Whitney, already had administrative duties. If Duverge were to be tried, the consulate would require some of McGowan's officers to sit as jurors. McGowan reluctantly agreed to detail four of his men to consular court duty, temporarily delaying his vessel's mission to China.[7] Additionally, he allowed Ensign V. O. Chase to serve as a prosecutor. Then, to the surprise of all observers except perhaps Duverge, McGowan volunteered to serve as counsel for the defense. As a naval officer, McGowan would have been well versed in legal proceedings. Like consular officers, captains were tasked with adjudicating cases far from American courtrooms. Accordingly, McGowan understood that, facing grave charges, Duverge must be afforded proper representation. Since no lawyer was available, the *Swatara*'s commander was the most competent option.

On June 26, Duverge was indicted for murder. Five days later, a trial was held inside the U.S. Consulate. Consul Campbell acted as judge and trier of law; the four officers from the *Swatara* constituted the jury and trier of fact. Ensign Chase prosecuted the case, and Commander McGowan represented Duverge. At 9:30 a.m., participants in the trial took their seats. Campbell swore in the jury and called the proceedings to order. He then asked Chase to call his first witness. Near simultaneously, the moon slipped in front of the sun.[8] For almost six minutes, the sky above tropical Tamatave turned black under an eclipse. When it was finished, the trial had started.

Daniel McDade testified about the circumstances surrounding the consular agent's death. He stated that he had spent the hours preceding the killing in Stanwood's tent. McDade claimed that around a quarter to eight o'clock, he and Stanwood heard a shot from the direction of Pargas's home. The two proceeded toward the house, the consular agent first sending a man to summon the Hova guards. Stanwood carried an unloaded revolver. Once in Pargas's yard, McDade could see movement inside, but "the light in the room was very dim." Duverge appeared. Stanwood demanded Cailleres, who was standing next to Duverge, be handed to him. When Duverge refused, Stanwood started to ascend the stairs. He told Duverge that he was going to arrest Cailleres. Duverge fired, sending Stanwood into McDade's arms, where he said, "Mr. McDade, I'm shot. Please take me out of here." McDade claimed Cailleres then shot Stanwood in the lower back.[9] Though McDade was steadfast that he had observed Duverge and then his brother-in-law shoot Stanwood, upon Commander McGowan's cross-examination, the witness allowed that he might not have been able to see other people who were present on account of darkness outside the house. McDade further admitted that his relations with Duverge "were not amicable." McGowan also gained from McDade a statement that Stanwood had not sworn out a warrant or given any reason that day to justify going to arrest Cailleres. McGowan asked McDade to indicate on a diagram where precisely he had been standing when Stanwood was first shot. When McDade asked to create his own diagram, McGowan objected. But Consul Campbell allowed the new diagram over the objection of Duverge's defense counsel. This was likely fortunate for the defense since subsequent witnesses would submit their own diagrams, each of which varied from the others, likely contributing to doubt amongst the jurors about the facts of the case.

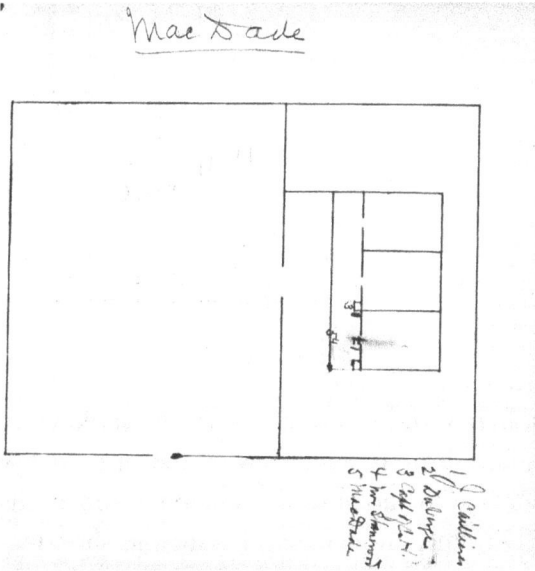

McDade's sketch

Campbell did not confine his work on the bench to ruling on objections. He also presented his own questions. Campbell asked McDade how far Stanwood had been from Duverge at the moment of the first shot. McDade answered that the two had been less than six feet apart. He added that Cailleres had fired as Stanwood was falling into McDade's arms. McDade also testified that "eight or nine shots" had been fired in total. All, in his opinion, had come from inside the house. According to McDade, Stanwood died fifteen minutes after the shooting. His final words were, "I want to know who fired that shot."

The next witness called was Henry Gass, Duverge's cabin boy. Gass's testimony was substantially the same as McDade's, though he annotated a diagram that indicated more witnesses were present at the shooting than McDade had stated. In addition to himself, the cabin boy remembered Madame Duverge and the three Hova guards at the scene of the killing.

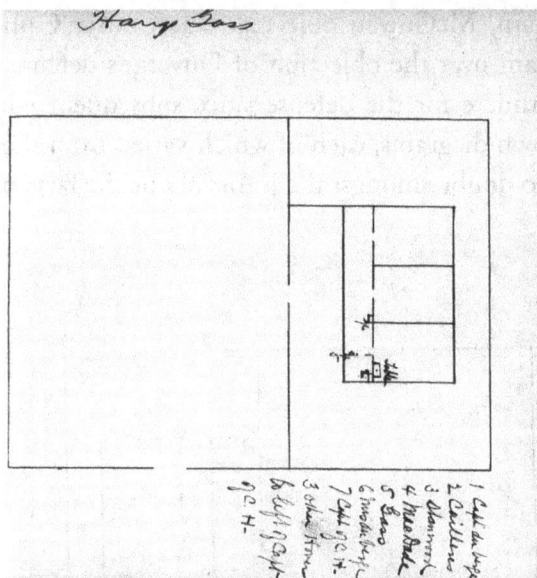

Gass's sketch

After Gass, James Middleton, the *Solitaire*'s cook, was called. In general, Middleton's testimony aligned with the prior two witnesses. But several statements were notable. Middleton claimed that Stanwood's comments to Duverge immediately before the shooting were slightly more extensive than previously stated. Middletown remembered Stanwood saying the following: "Now Captain DuVerge ever since you have been on this coast, there has been trouble now. You have come to a clinch and the law must have its course and according to law, I must arrest you or the boy until tomorrow morning."

Stanwood then spoke to the Hova captain in a language Middleton did not understand. When the Hova guard did nothing, Stanwood said in English that he would seize Cailleres. This conversation was slightly different from what was remembered by the other witnesses. Additionally, Middleton disclosed a conversation he claimed to have had with Duverge the morning of the killing, wherein he said, "Now look here Captain Du Verge, you can bet on what I say, Mr. Simmons and Mr. Stebbins, they are all working against you." When asked what caused him to make such a remark, Middleton stated the two had written "several letters" to Duverge, threatening him. He advised Duverge to give them the *Solitaire*, stating, "it isn't worth a damn." He also noted that

McDade had threatened Duverge. Middleton's statements damaged the credibility of McDade and the others. Middleton also submitted that it was nearly impossible to see that evening. The light inside Pargas's house was modest, and the moon was invisible at the time of shooting.[10] Middleton's diagram of the killing was similar to Gass's. He, too, remembered the Hova guards present and Madame Duverge to the left of Stanwood.

The testimony from Rainiganabelo, of the Hova Customs Office at Morondava, diverged from the previous witnesses. Rainiganabelo was the first witness to have no interest in the expedition. He clarified that Stanwood had not told him in Malagasy to arrest anyone, merely to "advance" into the house. He recalled that immediately prior to the shooting, Duverge had turned from Stanwood and extinguished the solitary lamp that provided light to the scene. The Hova later added that a second lamp on the table outside was also illuminated but did not give any significant light to the area of the shooting. Rainiganabelo testified that after Duverge had put out the light in the house, the foreigner then turned and fired at Stanwood. Cailleres jumped to stop Duverge from shooting again but himself was shot. Cailleres then stumbled to the side of the house and fled as Duverge continued firing. Another Hova, Captain Rinisonganahamy, testified that he was certain no one had been struck during the initial dispute between Duverge and Simmons earlier in the day. However, since a firearm had been discharged at that first ruckus when the Hovas visited Pargas's house later that evening, they all brought with them firearms. This statement contradicted McDade, Gass, and Rainiganabelo, who claimed none of the Hovas had been armed. Rabanasandrata, a Hova messenger assigned to the customs house, agreed with Rainiganabelo that Cailleres had been shot while trying to prevent Duverge from firing a second time at Stanwood. He then contradicted Captain Rinisonganahamy, claiming none of the Hovas were carrying firearms at the time of the killing. The final Hova, Randaranatova also stated no Hovas were armed, but offered no other remarkable testimony.

The prosecution then called James G. Field, assistant surgeon aboard the *Swatara*. His testimony, delivered in an appropriately clinical manner, related the otherwise ghoulish task of exhuming Stanwood's body and assessing the remains for the cause of death. Dr. Field shared that the corpse was in a "fair state of preservation" when he examined it on May

29, 1889. "The skeleton was intact, the skin on face, back, and limbs and abdomen was well preserved, that on the chest almost entirely gone, the beard hair and nails were as in life, the features good and did not show much evidence of decay."

Dr. Field noted the presence of a hole approximately three inches above the right abdomen. His impression was that the hole "gave the appearance as if caused by a bullet." He located a second hole in the "left back midway between the left shoulder blade and the spinal column, indicating the exit of a bullet."[11] Upon Chase's questioning, Dr. Field explained that the round that entered the abdomen was unlikely the same that exited the back. As Dr. Field described it, the first shot had torn open Stanwood's upper torso before exiting his back. A second shot had entered the abdomen just above the groin, presumably exiting through the gaping chest wound from the initial blast. Hence the presence of only two visible entry wounds: the first shot had destroyed the victim's chest and exited his back. The second had entered his abdomen at an angle and exited through the existing wound in the chest. McGowan asked if it was possible that a bullet had actually entered Stanwood's abdomen and exited his back, attempting to move responsibility from Duverge, who was above the victim, to one of the several people located on the steps below the consular agent. Dr. Field stated, "I do not think it possible for a ball entering the right abdomen to have so changed its course as to have made its exit so high as the spot designated in the left back," effectively ruling out the possibility that the shooter had been below Stanwood.

The physician also noted the trauma to a finger on Stanwood's right hand. McGowan tried to suggest that this injury indicated that some later opportunist had stolen a ring from the body, obliquely impugning the credibility of McDade or Middleton or one of the other witnesses who had guarded the corpse. But Dr. Field noted the wound was consistent with how the witnesses had reported quickly pulling Stanwood away from the scene of the shooting. The doctor also examined Joseph Cailleres. He related that a scar a half inch above the groin on the boy's left abdomen was consistent with a gunshot. There was no exit wound, suggesting the gun fired at Joseph had not been a large caliber weapon like that which had devastated Stanwood's chest. This strongly implied the presence of at least two different shooters.

The prosecution closed by offering a deposition from Jean Baptiste Pargas, who had been unwilling to travel to Tamatave. He had, however, agreed to have his testimony recorded by a French-speaking officer aboard the *Swatara* while it was anchored in Morondava. Pargas testified that he had seen Stanwood with a revolver. He heard words exchanged between Stanwood and Duverge in English and then someone fired. He claimed to have no other memory.

Commander McGowan then started direct examination of his only two witnesses: Joseph Cailleres and the accused.

The early part of Cailleres's testimony is notable because of his recollection of the dispute between Duverge and Simmons just before the shooting. Cailleres stated that Simmons mocked Duverge, telling him that he "could not navigate a vessel and that he had no more reputation in America than he had in Madagascar and that he was a great liar, and that none of them would believe him anymore." Cailleres claimed that Duverge responded that it did not matter. He had been working hard and would have the *Solitaire* back at sea in "twenty-five days." Simmons, though, according to Cailleres, told Duverge that Stanwood would prevent this because he and Stebbins were majority owners of the *Solitaire*. Duverge reminded Simmons that his name was not on the ship's articles. Duverge announced that, as captain, his loyalty was to the titleholders of the vessel, Dole and Flint. Simmons declared that Dole and Flint were "fictitious owners." It was at this point that the two began to fight.

Simmons's alleged comment about the possible invention of Dole and Flint is notable. It is striking that while Dole and Flint are listed in all extant documentation as the *Solitaire*'s owners, at no point did any person or corporation by that name ever file a claim to recover the ship. Further, the address for Dole and Flint provided by Duverge was the Exchange Building in Boston, which at the time of the drafting of the ship's articles was one of the city's largest and most celebrated office buildings. If one was seeking to give a generic address for a fictional corporation in Boston in 1887, the Exchange Building would have been a natural choice. It is possible then that Dole and Flint were a creation, an entity invented to allow Duverge to dupe his sailors into thinking they were participants in a grandiose expedition financed by wealthy Bostonians. However, the presence of B. Webb Dole, who had boarded in Boston to represent Dole and Flint and had then left the *Solitaire* in South Africa because of Duverge's abuse, suggested this was not the case. It is more likely that Simmons, if Cailleres's recollections are correct, merely accused Duverge of inventing Dole and Flint because he had been so misled by Duverge that he could no longer believe anything about the man. Similar to how he assumed Duverge had been ejected from Madagascar, which was inaccurate—Simmons had simply lost all faith in his former captain.

McDade, claimed Cailleres, also had no respect for Duverge. The boy recalled that one day he had accidentally brushed against McDade. The man told him, "You dirty little son-of-a-bitch of a Frenchman, I will kick your backside, because you do not look out for me." Duverge sprung to Cailleres's defense, saying, "If you want to touch that boy I will be there to lookout for him," to which McDade answered, "I will kick the two of you, because the one is no better than the other."[12]

Cailleres completely rejected the idea that Duverge shot Stanwood. Instead, Cailleres claimed that his sister shouted to her husband, "Louis, Louis, they are aiming at you!", at which point Stanwood shot Duverge in his leg and McDade fired at Cailleres, hitting the boy in the stomach. Cailleres stated that when the shooting started, the Hovas crashed through the exterior gate and ran away. Cailleres, now wounded, made his way back into the house through a side entrance. As he lay bleeding inside, he heard Middleton return and say, "Let us set fire to the house and drive the Captain out."

After his initial witness, McGowan called Duverge himself.

The accused was administered the oath and asked for his full name and shipmaster's certificate ("number 6444"). Duverge gave detailed testimony about his dispute with Simmons. What is most important from his memories of that early evening argument is the extent of injuries claimed by Duverge. He alleged that Simmons struck him with such force that it rendered Duverge unable to see from his right eye. Duverge claimed this was a further limit upon his already subpar vision. Ordinarily, he told the court, he wore spectacles. Without them, he could not see "beyond the distance of ten feet." This is the only recorded instance of Duverge ever mentioning eyewear. McGowan no doubt hoped the jury would interpret this injury as evidence that Duverge might have fired at Stanwood in error.

Duverge, like his brother-in-law, testified that at the time of Stanwood's killing, his wife warned him that both Stanwood and McDade were aiming at him. Duverge rushed inside the house, dodging a shot and grabbing a Joslyn rifle, from which he then fired a single round in the direction of muzzle fire he saw near Stanwood. He then went to retrieve more cartridges from inside the house. When he had "returned to the door everybody was gone." Duverge found Joseph grievously wounded in the back of the house. He instructed his wife to put cold water on the boy's wounds while Duverge located his double-barreled shotgun and revolver. He prevented his wife from lighting a lamp, warning her it would draw a further attack. Duverge heard more gunfire from near the southwest corner of the house. He wheeled one of his cannons outside to block the gate from being opened. He returned inside to try and lift the spirits of Cailleres, showing him that he, too, had been shot. Duverge then went outside to the veranda and hid underneath a table with his firearms, telling the court, "I was sure they would come back and fight again."[13] Duverge claimed that is precisely what happened.

Around midnight, two shots were fired at the front of the gate, followed by another series from an undetermined location outside. At four o'clock, more shots were fired, this time from the direction of Stanwood's tent. Duverge claimed he heard someone say, "Give us more pistols, we will go and take him out or set fire to the house." Other than the one round fired earlier from his rifle, he claimed to have fired no shots that evening. Duverge testified that the next morning an officer from the Hovas appeared, informing him "that he had taken the arms and the rum from the foreigners" and that there would be no more shooting.

The court asked Duverge to indicate where he had been shot. He showed a mark approximately six inches below his left knee on the outside of the leg. On the inside of the calf was a similar scar, which he claimed was the exit wound. His trousers and drawers were also presented to the court. Campbell took judicial notice that the tear to the trousers indicated a shot from the front. Dr. Field opined that the wound could have been from a gunshot.

Questioned about Simmons's alleged claim that Dole and Flint were nonexistent, Duverge claimed that the two had put $6,400 (approximately $220,000 in 2025) into the expedition. Asked to explain blood brothership, Duverge offered, "it consists of scratching your breast until you bleed, the other party does the same, a drop of each one's blood is put in a glass of rum or water: the native priest strikes the glass with an assegai [iron tipped spear]; which means you will be true to one another in sickness until death." He explained that the two aspiring brothers then drink the mixture. The bond created from the ceremony is, among the Sakalava, "as good as a passport and family."[14]

The court closed the questioning of Duverge by asking him to describe when he had discussed the expedition with Stanwood. Duverge related that he had only seen Stanwood twice before their reunion in Morondava in July 1888 and that the two had never before then discussed the Madagascar Trading and Development Company. He did, however, note that they had discussed the potential profitability of bringing a vessel from Boston to Madagascar.

The defense then faced the jury to provide a closing statement.

McGowan, commander of those jurors as well as the prosecutor, offered that he was not knowledgeable about the law. He lamented that Madame Duverge could not testify—the spousal privilege at that time regarded a wife incompetent to provide any testimony, unfavorable or otherwise, against her husband. This might have been a subtle way to introduce the explanation that Duverge had initially offered when he spoke with McGowan aboard the *Swatara*: that his wife had fired the fatal shot. Precluded by the rules of evidence from pursuing that defense, however, McGowan concentrated his attack in other areas. His first legal contention was that Stanwood had no authority to arrest Duverge because Duverge was then residing in the home of Pargas, a French resident. The Treaty of Commerce prohibited American consuls from entering the homes of foreigners. Further, while the treaty allowed consular agents to administer minor court proceedings, it did not permit traipsing about Madagascar, rounding up potential American criminals. McGowan cited the U.S. Consular Regulations for 1888 that read, "Consular Agents are not deemed to be judicial officers."[15] McGowan added that Stanwood was accredited to Andakabe, not the entire "West Coast" of Madagascar.

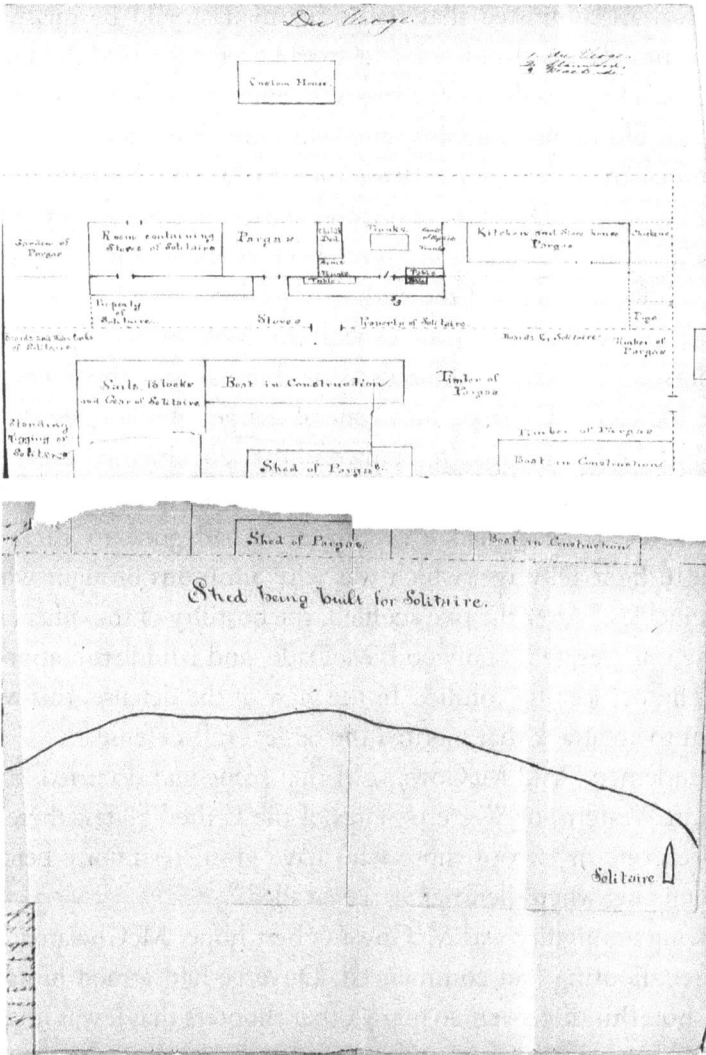

Duverge's sketch

The claims that Stanwood was acting outside his authority and outside of his jurisdiction gave credence to the suggestion that Duverge had acted in self-defense. Duverge had every reason to fear for his and his family's safety when Stanwood, armed with a pistol, appeared at the door. Having then "cleared away the cobwebs of this portion of the case," as McGowan put it, he moved onto an obvious administrative error: the indictment was for willful murder but failed to mention the place or the time of the death.

McGowan submitted that the indictment should be quashed and the case immediately dismissed. McGowan then addressed the substance of the case. He conceded that there was "enmity" between Duverge and Stanwood, Simmons, Stebbins, and McDade. But McGowan claimed the conflict emerged from a conspiracy to "annoy, humiliate, and, if possible, to crush" Duverge. Stanwood started the process by using his consular powers to dismiss the *Solitaire*'s crew. McGowan suggested that Stanwood not only lacked the authority to do so, but his true aim was to "cloak his designs" upon the expedition. McGowan emphasized that the claims of Simmons and Stebbins of abuse aboard the *Solitaire* gave few specific acts by Duverge, only general charges of misconduct. And he pointed to their own letters to Stanwood that documented Duverge had supplied them with generous supplies for their prospecting expedition.

It was clear, he argued, that Simmons had gone to Pargas's that evening to fight Duverge, which was why Simmons brought with him "false knuckles." After the two scuffled, the hostility of the others toward Duverge was elevated. Stanwood, McDade, and Middleton approached Pargas's home, seeking conflict. In the view of the defense, this was tantamount to an attack that merited the target's self-defense.

"Gentlemen," said McGowan, "if that scene had occurred in any of the South Western, or Western States of the United States, there would have been one or two of those who have given testimony before this Court, missing when their names were called."

Sowing ambiguity was McGowan's best hope. McGowan admitted that after shooting had commenced, Duverge had armed himself and fired a shot. But there were so many other shooters that it was impossible to place blame upon Duverge for Stanwood's death. Cailleres claimed to have seen Stanwood armed. Middleton, who had been recalled by the government to refute Duverge's claim that the accused had been shot by Stanwood or McDade, claimed that Duverge had been fired upon, but it was by his wife in error earlier in the evening. Middleton asserted she had shot Duverge while Simmons was on top of him and the two had struggled on the ground, in the confrontation before the encounter that led to Stanwood's death. McGowan claimed it was an unlikely scenario given Duverge's position underneath Simmons when the shot was fired.

"I must confess," McGowan said, "that I have wrestled with it without being able to solve it on any other hypothesis, than placing Mrs du Verge in a hole in the ground beneath the two combattants [sic]."

McGowan asked how it was that Duverge had been shot clean through, yet several minutes later, he appeared in the doorway to talk to Stanwood without any visible wound. But if Stanwood had shot him, McGowan offered, the matter was solved. Stanwood, as described by the witnesses and in several of the diagrams admitted as exhibits, had been standing in front of and to the left of Duverge. He was therefore below Duverge, which accounted for the wound as described by Dr. Field's initial assessment. As for Dr. Field's claim that he could rule out such a scenario, McGowan argued, "I do not believe that the science of surgery is so far advanced as to be infallible, nor do I believe the authorities quoted claim to be infallible."

McGowan did highlight one piece of Dr. Field's testimony, however. Near the close of the trial, Chase recalled Dr. Field to suggest that the two entry wounds on Stanwood's body might have been caused by Duverge's weapon. While Dr. Field allowed this point, he also stated that he had found three cartridges in the decedent's hip pocket. Chase was able to get Dr. Field to imply these cartridges were of a different round than those that had killed Stanwood, but McGowan reminded the jurors in his closing statement that there were not only varied accounts of who had shot whom, but even who had been armed. Stanwood, the prosecution admitted, was armed with a revolver. Both McDade and Middleton claimed, however, that the weapon was inert because it lacked a cylinder. Yet Stanwood was carrying cartridges in his pocket. As McGowan put it, when it came to deciding what had happened during the actual shooting, "I confess that the mass of conflicting testimony simply appalls me."[16] He hoped it would raise doubt among the jurors as well.

McGowan attempted to avoid any questioning of his own motivation in representing Duverge, taking a swipe at Campbell in the process. "Allusion has been made," he stated, "several times to my position as Counsel, as being of my own seeking. I acknowledge it." Apparently Campbell had attempted to sever any connection of loyalty between the commander and his men who were serving as jurors, attacking, at some unrecorded point, the commander's eagerness to defend Duverge.

McGowan responded that he had no choice but to serve as counsel for the accused. Duverge faced serious charges, could not afford his own attorney, and none had been provided by the government. "I could not stand by and see a man tried for murder, the most serious charge that could be brought against him, without making an effort to help him, and I do not believe the Government of the United States, would ever sanction the trial of a prisoner on a charge of this magnitude, without his having counsel." That striking comment highlights the possibility that McGowan volunteered to represent Duverge not just because of sympathy, but because he felt that without defense counsel the prosecution of Duverge was doomed to fail. McGowan summed up by conceding Duverge's many faults. "I do not consider the accused a good and blameless man. I go even further than that, I think he has put the talents that God gave him to base uses, and instead of being an honor to his family and friends; has so employed his talents, that they never care to hear him named, still, in this particular case where he is charged with murder, I do believe that he has been wrong."

This is likely a fair assessment of Duverge and the killing of Stanwood. Duverge was by no measure a moral man. At various times in his life, he was a liar, cheater, adulterer, mutineer, fraudster, traitor, and slaver. His expedition to Madagascar had been built upon misrepresentations and deceitfulness, funded by shady financing and unconscionable labor contracts. But there is considerable reason to doubt he shot Stanwood. The evening of the killing was dark, and the variety of opinions about who was and who was not present outside of Pargas's house raises significant questions about the chain of events that led to Stanwood's death. The most likely scenario is the one that comports with the court's eventual verdict.

Simmons and Duverge undoubtedly scuffled early in the evening. While the prosecution tried to suggest it was during that fight Duverge had been shot and that his wife was the shooter, this seems unlikely. Other than Middleton, none of the witnesses, including several who were oppositional to Duverge, reported the defendant's leg wounded at that time. After their fight, Simmons returned to Stanwood's tent, where the consular agent and McDade determined to confront Cailleres, who they believed had fired a shot. McGowan was right that Stanwood had no authority to do so. Stanwood's consular agent duties did not include running around Belo searching for French teenagers who might or might have not discharged a firearm. He simply lacked the authority to do so. Further, Duverge and his family were residing in the home of a Frenchman. McGowan had properly raised the absence of authority for an American consular officer to enter the home of a foreigner in Madagascar. But beyond that, the manner in which Stanwood chose to pursue Cailleres was reckless. The consular agent confronted a man who was at home with his family. Perhaps this is why Stanwood felt it necessary to carry a firearm to Pargas's house that evening, loaded or not. Both the defense and prosecution agreed that Stanwood was carrying *some* sort of a pistol, whether functional or not. The fact that Stanwood had cartridges in his pockets strongly suggests that the gun was in working order and that he was prepared to use it. Stanwood was intent on creating at least the appearance of a readiness to use lethal force. It seems likely that the first shot came from Duverge and that it struck Stanwood. The wound to Stanwood's chest was consistent with a close-range shot from a large-caliber weapon. All parties agree that the two men were standing near one another when the first shot was fired. And everyone who saw Duverge with a gun, except the defendant himself, witnessed him carrying a large revolver, just the sort of weapon that would blow a hole in a man's chest. Who was shot after that and how is immaterial to the charges against Duverge.

Under the common law then and today, murder is the unlawful killing of another human being with malice aforethought. Manslaughter is the unlawful killing of another human being without malice aforethought. The weight of the evidence removed any doubt that Duverge shot and killed Stanwood. While other shooters might have fired subsequent to Duverge's first round, it was his initial blast that killed the consular agent. However, it is impossible to conclude that Duverge's decision to shoot was made with malice aforethought. There is substantial evidence that suggests he was provoked into spontaneously shooting Stanwood in defense of himself and his family. It is undeniable that Duverge did not spend his evening planning to shoot Stanwood. As the sun set, the captain was chatting with Pargas outside. Simmons, apparently drunk, appeared and commenced mocking Duverge. Simmons, armed with metal knuckles, struck his former employer with such force that Duverge's eye was bloodied shut for months. Duverge then retreated to Pargas's house, with his wife, brother-in-law, and baby. Stanwood's appearance outside the Pargas home shortly after, surrounded by compatriots who had been drinking, must have alarmed Duverge. When he came to the door to address Stanwood, it would have been difficult, in the moonless night with a wounded eye, to see exactly who was standing before him. Perhaps, as Duverge claimed, he was able to make out that Stanwood was carrying a pistol. Wounded, unable to see properly, and confronted by a man who was yielding a gun, it is understandable that Duverge acted defensively.

On July 19, 1889, the jury returned a verdict of guilty on the lesser charge of manslaughter, determining that Duverge had "unlawfully and willfully but without premeditated malice" killed Consular Agent Stanwood. Consul Campbell sentenced Duverge to ten years' imprisonment and a fine of $100.[17] McGowan stated that Duverge would appeal to the secretary of state for a new trial on the grounds that the consul had failed to properly swear in witnesses, among other errors. If Duverge was hoping for McGowan's continued assistance, though, his hopes were misplaced. Commander McGowan returned to his ship that afternoon. Once aboard, he ordered immediate preparations for departure, their journey to China now foremost among his duties. At 3:25 the *Swatara* departed Tamatave, leaving Duverge and his family in the custody of Consul Campbell and Vice-Consul Whitney.[18]

CHAPTER NINE

The Unwanted Prisoner

McGowan's abrupt departure was unfortunate for Duverge. A competent representative would have found ample grounds for an immediate appeal.

As McGowan had noted before he fled Madagascar for China, the trial was riddled with procedural peculiarities and conflicts. The indictment did not specify where the alleged crime had occurred. Despite uncertainty that they did not understand the meaning of an oath, Campbell had sworn in the Hova witnesses. The jurors and the prosecutor were under the direct supervision of the defense counsel. The judge and the court reporter were the victim's colleagues. Additionally, as is often the case when military and diplomatic leaders are compelled to work jointly, a conflict of cultures between Campbell and McGowan created tensions that compromised the integrity of the tribunal. Commander McGowan, a Medal of Honor recipient who put duty before protocol, was of the opposite nature of Consul Campbell, who worked slowly, certain to adhere to every applicable bureaucratic requirement. When McGowan did not attend a Fourth of July celebration at the consulate, and then failed to display the French colors from the *Swatara* on Bastille Day, Campbell admonished him for a breach of official courtesies and wrote the State Department to complain. It was apparent from their exchanges that the two disliked one another, raising legitimate questions about their ability to administer a fair trial. Further, McGowan's counsel was less than sufficient. By his own admission, he was not knowledgeable about the law. Although experienced in matters of discipline at sea, he had no training in representing civilian defendants charged with murdering American officials in foreign lands. It was impossible for him to learn, from the limited legal resources available in the consulate's modest library and aboard the *Swatara*, the entirety of defenses available to his client. And Duverge's self-proclaimed limited English would have made it, in theory, difficult for the defendant to communicate with his representative.

Furthermore, there were important Constitutional questions about the conviction. The Fifth Amendment requires that "No person shall be held to answer for a capital, or otherwise infamous crime, unless on a presentment or indictment of a Grand Jury, except in cases arising in the land or naval forces." Duverge, not being then enlisted in the U.S. military, should only have been indicted by a grand jury, not Consul Campbell. Unless Duverge waived this right, the very indictment that charged him with murder was invalid. While the treaty with Madagascar established the rules of the consular court, no treaty can obviate a defendant's Constitutional rights. For this reason, American consular courts usually served merely as magisterial courts that tried only minor cases, referring more serious matters to courts in the United States.[1] In countries like China and Japan, which actually had standing American courts to try citizens and foreign sailors of American-flagged vessels, it was common to try felony cases. But even there, it was rare to actually carry out a serious sentence overseas. On seven occasions prior to Duverge's trial, consular courts had issued capital sentences.[2] But in only one of those cases was the sentence ever administered—an 1864 incident when a British citizen was hanged at the American Legation in Peking.[3] In the other six capital cases, all the convicted were granted clemency from execution and returned to the United States for incarceration, save one felon who committed suicide first. For these reasons, a new trial should have been granted. Duverge's conviction was manifestly unjust and merited review. However, with McGowan gone, he no longer had an advocate. It would be over a year until an appeal was filed on his behalf in Washington.

Campbell, meanwhile, had a prisoner to secure.

The same day the *Swatara* left Tamatave, the consul requested the Hovas provide a guard for Duverge. Campbell informed the Malagasy that the request was only until the prisoner could be transported to the United States. He then wrote to the State Department, asking for the urgent removal of Duverge. Anywhere other than a rented building next to the consulate would be better suited to incarcerate a convicted killer. An official at the State Department instructed that Campbell's request be sent to the U.S. Attorney General for action, but the American government took no immediate steps to resolve the Duverge matter.

The Hova government, however, was acting swiftly upon a request from Campbell to address lawlessness in the western part of the island. In September, Antananarivo sent forces to establish order along Madagascar's southwest coast. Campbell opined, "It is now more than probable that since the affair of the 'Solitaire' a stricter surveillance will be kept upon American vessels."[4] Campbell also noted that the Hovas lacked any significant naval power, their forces at sea being limited to one steamer, canoes and pirogues, and a complete absence of any government harbor pilots.[5] Despite such shortcomings, Antananarivo honored his request for a response, which Campbell applauded in correspondence to Washington. A month later, however, he was forced to reverse his enthusiasm after he learned that the Hovas were not only being pushed back on the west coast, but that a vessel from Boston had recently arrived, bringing with it between five hundred and six hundred barrels of illicit gunpowder for the Sakalavas.

Sympathy for Duverge came from Connecticut, where, in August 1889, Captain B. J. Merryman of Fairhaven wrote to Campbell. Merryman claimed that Stanwood had swindled him of several thousand dollars through "a fraudulent transaction which happened in New Zealand some years ago."[6] Merryman was almost certainly the owner of the barque *Courier*, the vessel Stanwood allegedly misappropriated in Wellington. Commenting upon Duverge's trial in his letter, he wrote: "My sympathy is wholly with Capt DuVerge as I know something of the Consul he was dealing with. I am surprised that such a man was employed by the U.S. Government."[7]

Campbell was less concerned about Stanwood's transgressions than Duverge's continued presence in Tamatave, a dilemma about which Washington seemed unable to find a solution. In August, the acting attorney general advised the State Department that "as there was no statute which authorized the imprisonment in the United States of a person convicted by a consular court, the removal of Du Verge to the

United States for that purpose would be unlawful."[8] This information unknown to Campbell at the time, he sent yet another desperate despatch in October, proclaiming: "In reference to Duverge I wish to inform the Department that the sooner something definite will be done as to his removal from here the better." He noted that Vice-Consul Whitney, presently acting as Duverge's marshal, was scheduled to return to the United States for a year.

The State Department's response was that until a decision was reached about the prisoner's possible removal, "Duverge should be subjected to prison discipline, at least to the extent of seeing that he is not provided with a revolver or means of escape." Such measures would have been obvious to Campbell, who was well aware of the convict's nature. He emphasized this risk to the State Department in his next despatch, stating, "Duverge's history and character are so treacherous and bad that I fear if he is left here much longer he may give more trouble, particularly as his confinement seems to grow daily more irksome and monstrous to him." Concurrently, Duverge complained of his health. He claimed he could not stop coughing and requested a doctor. He also asked for a visit from a lawyer. Both were allowed.[9]

While Washington's interest in Stanwood faded, the affair consumed Campbell. In December, he sent a ten-page rambling and confused explanation of why he had not received and responded to the consular agent's messages about the chaotic southwest. An internal State Department note on the despatch reads, "I cannot make anything out of this jumble." Officials in Washington were no longer vexed by Stanwood's allegations, let alone why Campbell might or might not have been unresponsive.

When Vice-Consul Whitney returned to the United States, Duverge was left guarded only by Hovas. Campbell informed the State Department that this was insufficient, as he considered the guards untrustworthy. He emphasized that individuals in Tamatave might attempt to help Duverge escape. After learning Duverge was a Mason and that he had appealed for assistance from the local brotherhood, Campbell consulted with a senior Mason who assured the consul that, by virtue of Duverge's conviction, no aid would be forthcoming. But Campbell feared his prisoner was cultivating other accomplices. A "fugitive creole" from Mauritius attempted to visit Duverge but was turned away. Campbell cautioned the

State Department that Duverge was an accomplished traveler who could disappear at any moment and invent a new life someplace else, though likely not America. The prisoner, Campbell submitted, was known from "Maine to Oregon" because of "unpaid bills." Campbell alone could not be expected to maintain Duverge.

Nor could he be expected to be responsible for the prisoner's family. Joseph Cailleres had returned to France of his own volition following the trial, but Marie Duverge and her young daughter remained with her husband. Their presence was costly for the consulate and added to sympathy among certain locals for Duverge. This was especially true because, according to Campbell, Madame Duverge appeared "very likely to become a mother in another month or six weeks time." Duverge, who by December was writing Campbell almost daily with demands, requested a French- or English-speaking servant to help him and his growing household. This was denied.

In January 1890, the Hova guards moved the Duverge family from their ad hoc jail next to the vice-consul's house to a building next to the consulate. This at least was situated somewhat closer to a government battery, where there were numerous Hova soldiers. The change also spared Campbell the inconvenience of crossing town to visit Duverge every time he sent a note about feeling sick or needing to discuss the terms of his incarceration. A week later, Campbell appointed John Dublin as a Marshal of the Consular Court. Unknown to Campbell until recently, Dublin was an elderly black American who somehow had ended up in Tamatave. He informed Duverge that Dublin was his new and sole interlocutor with the consulate, stating, "Any further business you may have with the U.S Consul, or the Consul with you, will be done through the Marshal."[10]

Among such business was a slew of requests for meetings with lawyers and doctors, all of which Campbell approved. A team of physicians examined the prisoner on January 13, 1890, and declared him fit despite Duverge's claims of declining health. Campbell considered him to be malingering and wrote the State Department that the threat of escape remained a concern. He emphasized that Tamatave was full of fugitives from Mauritius and that "their conduct and morals are as black as some of their skins."[11] He also renewed concerns about Madame Duverge, who he claimed "might as well be called the leading lady in the tragedy." His worries originated from Marie Duverge's vigorous efforts to elicit sympathy from anyone who would listen. In exchange for permission to stay with Duverge, Madame Duverge had agreed to send all of her correspondence to Campbell before transmission to third parties. However, the consul uncovered in early 1890 that Marie had been covertly passing letters to Elixa Watts, the wife of an American captain whose vessel was then visiting Tamatave. Mrs. Watts had become obsessed with the Duverge case. Marie pleaded with Mrs. Watts to, upon her return to America, "say well to those who would speak to her of Madagascar that there was an innocent man here after being robbed of all he possessed, suffering more than an unjust condemnation, by a consul in order to please his friends."[12] Watts transmitted money to Marie and insisted Madame Duverge and her daughter visit the Watts home when they eventually reached the United States. In one exchange, Marie sent a letter of thanks to Watts including in it some ostrich feathers she had procured during the *Solitaire*'s stop in South Africa. In another letter, Marie told Watts that she looked at her photograph regularly and thought, "this is the only woman who had pity on me and my child." To draw further sympathy, she remembered to Watts the Duverge child who had died the previous November and how his body had finally been returned for burial in the "repository of my family in Bordeaux."[13] Presumably the remains had been sent back to France with Joseph Cailleres. Campbell, learning of these secret conversations between the ladies, summoned Captain Watts, who shut down the correspondence.

Though Elixa Watts was then removed from Marie Duverge's life, she soon had other distractions, as in March she gave birth to a son. Duverge's improvised prison now held him, his wife, his three-year-old daughter, and a newborn. Campbell formalized an agreement with the Hovas to hold the prisoner in the Tamatave fort, but funding was required. He wrote to the State Department for assistance. The plan was only a temporary solution in Campbell's view, as the Hova government considered Duverge "disreputable and has for some time" and would not keep him for the duration of his sentence. Of particular offense to the local authorities was how, after his dismissal from Queen's Ranavalona III's army, Duverge departed Antananarivo and "took a young Hova girl along with him, whom he afterwards abandoned."[14] Nevertheless, Campbell asked the State Department for $600 (approximately $20,000 in 2025) to pay the Hovas so Duverge might be incarcerated somewhere more suitable than in a residence next to the consulate. Assistant Secretary of State William F. Wharton responded that attempts were being made to address the situation but that, in the meanwhile, Campbell should "do his best under the law" to maintain the prisoner.[15]

The prisoner was keeping himself occupied sending notes to Campbell, demanding improved conditions and medicine. Additionally, he requested that he be allowed to file a claim for the *Solitaire*. Duverge submitted that the ship was worth approximately $24,000 ($800,000 in 2025). Included in its inventory was a "photographic apparatus complete and 12 dozen dry plates." Duverge further claimed the loss of trade from the affair was $150,000 (approximately $4 million in 2025).[16] No further news was recorded of the vessel after Stanwood's death. It is likely that Duverge's Sakalava blood brothers, knowing that chances of his return were remote, scavenged what they could from the ship and then left her remains along the beach. Before long, the tides and weather would have eliminated most of the ship. Stanwood's possessions in Andakabe were auctioned by the Hova governor, yielding $195 (approximately $6,500 in 2025). The balance was remitted to Consul Campbell.[17] Two years after Duverge's arrival on the west coast, the only traces of the *Solitaire* would have been a collection of wood in the sand. The only evidence of former consular agent Stanwood would have been his grave, now forgotten but likely situated someplace in Morondava.

In June, Marie Duverge wrote to Secretary of State James G. Blaine. She requested passage for herself and her children, then three years old and three months old, to France. As Madame Duverge courted the support of Secretary Blaine, Duverge's allies in America started their own efforts to liberate the convicted killer. Ferdinand C. Poree, an attorney in Boston, had taken up the case. A fellow veteran of the Massachusetts 30th, Poree and Duverge had overlapped service for about six months, the future lawyer concluding his wartime experience in March 1865.

In August 1890, Poree submitted an appeal to Secretary Blaine, outlining the flawed process that had resulted in Duverge's conviction as well as the inhumane condition in which his client was presently

incarcerated. He commenced with a confident recitation of the benevolent and courageous life Duverge had led before his arrest. The description was so hyperbolic that it could only have originated from the prisoner himself.

> Capt. L. de R. du Verge, who as an officer served with credit to
> himself and regiment (the 30th Mass. Inft. Vols.) in the War of
> the Rebellion; who paid the passage in gold of 120 men, to aid in
> suppressing the same, from Mauritius to New York City;
>   Who rather than sanction the decapitation of some French soldiers
> taken by her Majesty's troops (the Queen of the Hovas, Madagascar)
> resigned his commission as colonel of the Northern Division of the
> Island;
>   Who was wounded in rescuing three priests from slow death by
> natives upon the Congo, Africa;
>   Who plunged into the China Seas when mate of a vessel to rescue
> a man from downing, —
>   This man, an AMERICAN CITIZEN, that served the nation as
> an officer during the Rebellion, and as a Consul at the Port of St. Paul
> de Loando, Africa, is now confined in a grass house, located near a
> stagnant marsh, that poisons the breath of his nostrils, ill and sore
> and covered with lice, without medical attendance, guarded by Hovan
> soldiers, within the consular jurisdiction of John P. Campbell, Consul
> at Tamatave, Madagascar.

Poree then turned to the circumstances of Stanwood's death, which
by his account was the fault not of his client, but of the consular agent.
The attorney argued that Duverge had acted in self-defense. Stanwood,
claimed Poree, had entered Duverge's temporary home "at night with ten
armed men" before one of the men "summarily strikes Capt. du Verge in
the eye, blinding him, and the man Stanwood draws his pistol and shoots
him in the leg. Captain du Verge then opens fire, shooting and killing
Stanwood." By Poree's description, Duverge's conduct was entirely justified. However, "for thus defending his life and property," Duverge was
indicted for murder and forced to appear before a consular court where
"after going through the forms of a trial" he was sentenced to pay a fine of

$100 and serve ten years in "such prison or penitentiary as the Hon. Secretary of State shall designate for 'Manslaughter without premeditated malice.'" Poree closed by arguing that since Duverge had been charged only with murder, he should not have been convicted of the lesser offense of manslaughter. Failing that argument, he submitted, Duverge should be permitted to serve his sentence in America.

He supplemented this formal appeal with a collection of addendums that supported his client's character. These included a lengthy letter from Duverge to his old benefactor, General Rolland, to whom he had dedicated his 1887 book. In this letter, Duverge offered his friend his version of Stanwood's killing, which was essentially the same tale Poree related in the aforementioned appeal. Also included were multiple letters of reference from his former compatriots of the 30th Massachusetts, a letter of support from General Rolland, a note from Poree's co-counsel in Washington that recorded a meeting with President Benjamin Harrison's secretary Elijah W. Halford, various news clippings from Madagascar about the affair, and an 1894 hand-drawn map of Tamatave that indicates the location of the consulate and Duverge's place of incarceration.

Despite this appeal and efforts to gain a pardon from President Harrison, neither Duverge nor Campbell heard anything further about his release or removal to the United States. Campbell requested additional funds for Duverge's trial and continued detention next to the consulate. While the State Department granted this support, the $600 Campbell had requested to house the prisoner in the Hova fort was not approved. This was likely because of the attorney general's concerns that neither of the two treaties between Washington and Antananarivo obligated the Hovas to keep American prisoners. Encouraging the Malagasy to detain Duverge, an American, might establish a precedent that would erode protections for other U.S. citizens. Additionally, the attorney general issued an advisory opinion that eliminated any possibility of Duverge being sent to America in the near future. That opinion informed the State Department that the comments of the acting attorney general a year earlier were correct: there was no authority under U.S. law to remove Duverge to an American prison. When the State Department enquired if the prisoner might be transferred to existing consular detention facilities in Egypt or China, the attorney general declared that this, too, was not permitted. However, the attorney general's office advised that the matter had been referred to Congress for a potential legislative solution.

Campbell continued his complaints to Washington. One problem was that Vice-Consul Whitney had failed to return after a year. Whitney was still in America, arranging for work with a British trading house in Madagascar, confidentially telling the State Department that Campbell was a slow and often ineffective consul. He was missed in Tamatave. The lack of a vice-consul, Campbell protested, made his work impossible. Campbell stressed that, for a year and a half, other than the assistance of an "old colored man who brings the prisoner food," he had had no help securing Duverge. He complained about the lack of information from the secretary of state, writing that a lack of action "embarrasses and depresses" him. Further, his perceived inability to resolve the matter put him at a disadvantage before Hovan authorities, a dangerous proposition for a diplomat, especially in light of the "present unsettled political state of the country."

And the reasons to keep Duverge under a close watch continued.

At the start of 1891, Captain Dowson, a representative of the Madagascar Mercantile and Development Syndicate, appeared at the consulate and asked to meet with Duverge. The London-based company was led by Major General Edward Anson, the former governor of the Straits Settlements who had adventured in Madagascar in the early 1860s. The Syndicate had recently secured a timber concession from the Hovas, possibly on the claim of the earlier Lambert Charter. Dowson informed Campbell that the grant was worth $3 million (over $100 million in 2025). Campbell, however, believed the claim was worthless because of certain stipulations on the concession from the Hovas. The land at issue included an area of western Madagascar about which, claimed Captain Dowson, Duverge was "intimately familiar." For this reason, he sought an interview with the prisoner. Campbell informed Dowson that this was impossible and sent him away.[18] It seems likely that Dowson was attempting to buy out Duverge's existing grant of land on the west coast. Very likely the Hovas told the Syndicate that until all titleholders transferred their interests to Anson's company, the concession would not be honored. In any event, the grant was likely unexploitable because of

Sakalava unrest. By March, Campbell recorded the trouble was now a "serious uprising and disturbance" against Hova attempts to secure the west coast.

Any leniency Campbell might have held for his prisoner was gone by February 1891. On February 24, Duverge transmitted a somber message to Marshal Dublin: "My child is dead and I beg you in the name of humanity to ask the consul to allow me (under your care) to attend its funeral when such will take place." Dublin dutifully passed the message to Campbell. The consul responded to Dublin, through whom all messages to Duverge had been sent since the Marshal's appointment, "I can find no authority that would admit of my granting the U.S. prisoner L. Rathier du Verge the request made by him upon the consulate."[19] Consul Campbell was then informed that his replacement, John L. Waller, would travel to Madagascar from the United States in May. Campbell wrote Washington that he would remain in Tamatave until Waller's arrival, citing "important matters to discuss" with the new consul. Certainly among those matters was the maintenance of Duverge, who was still secured in his makeshift cell next to the consulate, guarded by Hova soldiers and serviced by Marshal Dublin. Missionary J. A. Holder, who had first encountered Duverge in August 1884 when he had arrived to join the Hova fight against the French, recalled seeing the prisoner before and following the trial.

> In July, 1889, I was called to render some assistance in connection with the trial of Captain du Verge, the man I had met on the road from the coast to the capital, at the head of his small army of volunteers during the war. He had shot and killed a Mr. Stanwood, the US representative on the west coast and was accused of murder. He was brought to Tamatave by the U.S. Swatam [*sic*] and tried at the American consulate. The Rev. A. Hewlett of the S. P. G. [Society for the Propagation of the Gospel in Foreign Parts, a nineteenth-century Church of England missionary institution] was engaged to translate the evidence of native witnesses and I was retained by Captain McGowan, who conducted the defence, to check his translations; although neither of us, I believe, received any fee for our services. It was a tedious business lasting several weeks and interfering sadly

with our work. In the end the man was convicted of manslaughter and sentenced to ten years imprisonment but the curious thing about it was that the culprit was not taken away by the ship to be imprisoned in America; he was confined in a small house in the town and guarded by native soldiers. I often used to see him sitting at the door as I passed by, and sometimes I had the opportunity of conversing with him and lending him books. I am under the impression, however, that after a while he was either taken away to be incarcerated elsewhere or released altogether.[20]

Houlder's impression was incorrect.

On June 6, 1891, Louis Duverge died of a "Stroke of serious apoplexy" while imprisoned in Tamatave.[21] He had served one year, nine months, and seventeen days of his ten-year sentence.

CHAPTER TEN

The End of the Century

Despite the proclamation of a team of doctors six months earlier that the prisoner was "fit," Duverge had been in ill health for months, if not years, before his death. This was expected, considering his history. Although he was a chronic malingerer, feigning illness when beneficial, Duverge had experienced an undeniably trying life. If General Rolland was to be believed, Duverge had survived dangerous combat in Europe and North Africa, a likely claim considering the location and length of his service with the French. If Duverge was to be believed, he had survived dangerous combat in America, an unlikely claim considering the location and length of his service with the Union. But while Duverge had lived comfortably for most of his time in America, much of his experience abroad was profoundly hazardous. He was shot in the hand in Congo and, years later, in the leg in Madagascar, preceded of course by a vicious wounding of his eye. Duverge's work as a mariner, where he managed difficult ships and difficult men, was physically and mentally draining. Throughout his time in Africa, he suffered fevers and accompanying delusions and digestive problems endemic to the tropics. His pattern of wanton womanizing made it a near certainty that his body was riddled with venereal disease. Given Duverge's life of anxiety, trauma, poor nutrition, and sickness, it is entirely understandable that he died at fifty-one.

Sudden death was common in Madagascar. Two years later, Vice-Consul Whitney, who returned to Tamatave to work for a British trading firm, died of unknown causes. Charles Stebbins, one of Duverge's crew members aboard the *Solitaire*, died of an unknown illness in Morondava a few weeks after Stanwood's death. And, of course, the two Duverge children perished in Madagascar.

In the days following the prisoner's death, Campbell heard rumors that Duverge had been poisoned. Probably rightly, he dismissed these allegations in communications to the State Department. The Hova government had no pressing need to kill Duverge in 1891 because he was no longer a threat. The relationships Duverge cultivated in Madagascar had frayed beyond the point of utility. Both the British and French, though previously disquieted about Duverge, would not have worried about him enough to have him killed. And the American government in the late 1800s was barely engaged in diplomacy, let alone assassination. The same was true of Campbell and his employee, Marshal Dublin. Both had direct access to Duverge and could have arranged for the prisoner to be poisoned. Duverge's incarceration was an unwanted and unpleasant obligation for Campbell, who, from conviction onward, sought to have the prisoner moved elsewhere. Duverge's death would have lessened that burden. But by June 1891, it was known to Campbell that his time with Duverge was soon to end, and he had become tired of work in general. Consul Waller was only days away. Campbell had no more incentive to eliminate Duverge than Dublin, whose employment was contingent on Duverge's survival. Perhaps some other personal conflict might have led to Duverge's poisoning, maybe some former associate from Mauritius or elsewhere had the prisoner killed. But if so, it took them almost two years to do it, more than long enough for Duverge to have sold out a former conspirator in exchange for release or improved conditions. Most likely, Duverge was simply an aging, impoverished, depressed, sick man who finally succumbed to an adventurous but damaging life.

The final legal action involving Duverge occurred in 1894 when an attorney filed for a pension on behalf of Marie Duverge and her daughter, Duverge's only known living child. That pension was never paid, possibly because Marie remained in France and was unable to pursue the claim.

A month after Duverge's death, Consul John L. Waller arrived in Tamatave. Consul Campbell then departed for the Riviera to recover his health before returning home. In December 1891, he returned to Washington and disposed of Stanwood's "watch, chain, shirt studs, opera glasses, and badge." The $45 realized from the sale (approximately

$1,400 in 2025) was remitted to the State Department. There is no further record of the disposition of his estate.

Consul Waller's tenure in Madagascar was the capstone of an extraordinary life that saw him rise from slavery to diplomacy. Born in Missouri in 1850, he was emancipated in 1865, after which he moved to Iowa and taught himself law. He passed the state bar exam, practicing for several years before moving to Kansas. There, he entered the newspaper business. In 1888, he served as the first black presidential elector. President Benjamin Harrison awarded Waller a consular appointment to Tamatave. Consul Waller developed a close relationship with the Hova authorities, so much so that his daughter later married Queen Ranavalona III's nephew. Remaining in Madagascar after his consul tenure ended in January 1894, the queen granted him a concession of 150,000 acres in the southwest, likely to undermine French claims to the island. Waller then set about establishing a racially tolerant enclave for black American emigres, an ambition he had held since the first days of his arrival in the country. The project was named "Wallerland." After the second Franco-Hova War started in late 1894, Waller sent his wife, his daughter, and his new grandson, Andriamanantena Paul Razafinkarefo, to New York.[1]

Waller, meanwhile, faced danger in Madagascar. Unlike their previous campaign, the French in this war committed significant resources to conquering the island. French marines and soldiers quickly captured Tamatave and Mahajanga and then launched a year-long drive to Antananarivo. In September 1895, the capital fell. After centuries of resistance, the Hovas finally succumbed to European domination. Initially, Paris sought to maintain the appearance of Hova control over Madagascar. The French entertained this mirage because Queen Ranavalona III's government seemed easy to manipulate. The commanding French general at the time reported, "the Hova Government appeared very eager to satisfy us."[2] This course, however, was soon reversed. A newly installed French resident assumed most of the duties previously held by the Hova monarchy and, in 1897, Queen Ranavalona III was exiled, ending Hova rule permanently.

When Hova rule disappeared, so did protections for former consul Waller. This included from his own consulate. Newly arrived Consul

Edward Telfair Wetter, appointed by President Grover Cleveland, was the son of a slaveholder. He harbored no goodwill toward John Waller and his planned Wallerland. As Waller was preparing to return to America in October 1894 to seek support for his project, Wetter arrested him. Wetter accused the former consul of mishandling the estate of an American who had died in Madagascar during Waller's tenure. He then convened a rushed consular court to try the matter. Wetter, who served as judge before four local American jurors, found Waller liable for a breach of fiduciary duty and ordered him to pay $1,964.62 (approximately $70,000 in 2025).[3] In March 1895, the French arrested Waller for espionage, subjecting him to a tribunal that made Wetter's kangaroo court look like a model of due process. The proceedings, hidden from the public and conducted in French with only a hint of legal representation for Waller, resulted in a sentence of twenty years hard labor. After the fall of Antananarivo, Waller was sent to France to serve his time. Following months of pressure from the Cleveland Administration, Waller was finally released and sent home to America in 1896.[4]

Concurrently, Washington moved to end further consular courts in Madagascar. In May, the State Department, at the insistence of the French Ambassador in Washington, instructed Consul Wetter to "suspend until further instructed the exercise of consular judicial function in all cases where cooperation of an established French court is available for disposition of judicial cases affecting Americans." Soon after, American consular officers in Zanzibar, where a British protectorate had recently been established, received similar instructions. The American Consulate in Cairo was similarly instructed after the British formalized a so-called "veiled protectorate" over Egypt. It was no longer necessary to offer Americans in these locations special legal venues.

Duverge's rise and Stanwood's fall would not be possible in today's world of American diplomacy. At the most basic level, they never would have been hired. From the newest consular officer to the most well-connected ambassador, every American diplomat today is subject to an extensive background investigation and suitability review. That review would preclude the hiring of someone of Duverge's character—or even Stanwood's, with his history of fraudulent behavior. The protection of diplomats is also far more sophisticated now than in Stanwood's day.

Presently, all but a handful of American diplomatic missions are secured by multiple Diplomatic Security Service special agents and a detachment of United States Marine security guards. Subtle (and sometimes secret) but effective measures exist to protect personnel who venture outside of diplomatic facilities as well. No consular officer in 2025 would charge off with a firearm to intervene in a violent dispute between American citizens. If they needed to involve themselves in such a dangerous matter, there would be others with guns to protect them.

Equally impossible to imagine today is a form of American diplomacy that is as humble, and perhaps naive, as what existed in the late 1800s. The United States was no doubt an ascendant power when Duverge landed in Stanwood's consular district in 1888. The annexation of Hawaii a decade later would secure all of the territory that now constitutes the fifty states. At the close of the century, America was a massive country with massive potential that was being developed quickly. The nation's transition from an agricultural to a multifaceted economy was moving rapidly and bringing its growing population along with it. Railroads intersected the newly united continent, connecting burgeoning cities to the riches of the west and ports on both coasts. New Americans from old countries grew the population in new places. Foreign trade was changing but always increasing. As kerosene eroded the demand for whale oil, American vessels stopped carrying harpoons and shifted to carrying cargo. Supported by consular officers in far-flung ports, an explosion of foreign commerce accompanied America's domestic growth. American products competed strongly with European offerings, incentivizing financiers to send an increasing number of vessels from Boston, New York, and San Francisco to locations farther and farther afar. The demand for exotic raw materials in the United States encouraged a healthy return trade that contributed further to economic growth. Promoting that exchange was the work of consular officers ready to act as neutral arbiters, and aid countrymen seeking to make a profit and send the proceeds back home.

In this spirit of cooperative and mutually beneficial trade, American diplomacy thrived in the late 1800s. There were minor U.S. interventions abroad. The Mexican-American War, of course, was a significant extension of American power. There were incursions in Latin America. But unlike the European states, which had divided Africa and much of the rest of the world among a handful of countries, for most of the nineteenth century, the United States was content to keep the peace in the Western Hemisphere and pursue elsewhere prosperity through trade over political dominance. This would end in 1898 when the Spanish-American War saw American forces fighting not only in the Caribbean but also the Philippines, where the United States acquired its first significant colony.

Recently it has become fashionable to contend that minor American action overseas prior to the Spanish-American War amounted to colonialism, but the evidence is specious. Before that conflict, America was simply more interested in the dollar than domination, and most Americans shirked using the federal government to exploit foreigners. The Guano Islands Act that Duverge aspired to invoke in a claim over Europa Island is sometimes alluded to for evidence of some sort of proto-American colonialism. But the underlying purpose of that statute was to empower individual Americans to exploit isolated islands for phosphate deposits, not the federal government or some sort of quasi-governmental company. The United States government, prior to 1898, never embarked on ambitious crusades to install American officials running foreign states, let alone sponsored religious missionaries who were intent on converting indigenous populations overseas. As one academic reviewing the historical record assessed, "The Malagasy had seen that the U.S., faithful to their tradition of freedom, had no designs on the island whatsoever and neither did they want to become involved in internal matters."[5]

The period of Stanwood's death holds value as a caution against the danger of unnecessary intervention. British and French meddling in Madagascar was a constant, costly skirmish between two powers. The British probably fared best, managing to minimize Paris's influence over the country for two centuries until later agreeing to French domination of Madagascar in exchange for concessions in North Africa. France held Madagascar from Antananarivo's fall in 1895 until 1942, when the allies defeated the Vichy presence. After the war, the Fourth Republic controlled the island until an independence referendum in 1958. The United States, meanwhile, continued to largely ignore Madagascar. During Stanwood's era, this was because of a deliberate policy of non-interference. Even during the twentieth century, when American foreign policy experienced a rapid shift toward interventionism, Madagascar's geographic isolation and location within the Francosphere isolated it from the persuasion exerted by Washington on other developing states.

Stanwood, in a way, suffered the fate of excessive interventionism. He had no power that night in Belo, to arrest Joseph Cailleres, who was not an American citizen. There was no need to visit the home of a foreigner, in contravention of Stanwood's consular authorities. This is not to say Duverge did not kill the consular agent. It seems near certain that he did. But Duverge likely had a valid claim to self-defense. Had Stanwood not gone to Pargas's house that evening, the affair most probably would have concluded in a less dramatic manner. Perhaps the next day, Stanwood would have forgotten the scuffle between Duverge and Simmons and continued his gradual dissolution of the Madagascar Trading and Development Company. Perhaps the *Solitaire* would have eventually been refloated and returned to Boston. Perhaps Duverge would have become angry but not murderous, and again disappeared into the forest, leaving behind another wife and puzzled colleagues. But what did happen was that Victor Stanwood died on a dark night under a sliver of a moon in front of a beachside house from Louis Duverge's gun.

The shooting killed both of them, in a manner: Stanwood immediately from trauma, Duverge later from incarceration.

Duverge's remains were interred in the Tamatave cemetery *pour étrangers*. That cemetery, situated near the water in a coastal town, has been hammered by countless storms and monsoons in the 130-odd years since Duverge died. Today, most of the graves are recent, having been placed on top of the deteriorated remains of previous internments. One section in the northeast of the cemetery includes a handful of late nineteenth-century markers. Only two are still completely readable, neither of which belong to Duverge. One headstone, however, with only the outline of an "L" at the start of some otherwise indecipherable text, is consistent with where Louis Leopold Du Rothier Duverge would have been buried. Perhaps his remains are there, buried on the opposite side of the island from Victor Stanwood.

The killer lived for two and a half years after his victim's death, but Duverge's adventures once he surrendered to the *Swatara* were finished. Confined, he was barely alive. Duverge's existence, like Stanwood's, was

Author at Duverge's possible grave in Tamatave (Toamasina), Madagascar

centered on freedom. During an era when danger and individualism were the quickest paths to honor and fortune, Duverge lived fearlessly and independently. He had no shortage of faults, but his energy and escapades are notable as a matter of curiosity and historical insight.

Victor Stanwood, however, should be remembered for more profound reasons. While likely not as unscrupulous as Duverge, he was not free of sin. But Stanwood's conduct in attempting to alert his superiors to the slave trade in western Madagascar, no matter his motivations, was commendable. And though he might have erred in how he investigated the *Solitaire* case, he certainly did not deserve to die.

It is known that *Solitaire* crew member Charles Stebbins was buried in Morondava in a grave surrounded by a small fence. It is unknown where Stanwood's body was laid to rest after its exhumation, but perhaps it is near that of Stebbins. If Stanwood's grave could be identified, it would seem fitting that it be suitably marked to commemorate a man who died in the service of his country, at the hand of a man who lived a remarkable though devious life.

AFRICAN FEVER
MONROVIA LIBERIA 1882
JESSE H MOORE
YELLOW FEVER CALLAO 1883
DAVID T BUNKER
YELLOW FEVER DEMERARA 1886
VICTOR F W STANWOOD
MURDERED MADAGASCAR 1888
WILLIAM D McCOY
FEVER MONROVIA LIBERIA 1893
JOHN R MEADE
YELLOW FEVER
SANTO DOMINGO 1894

Stanwood's memorial plaque today, inside the Department of State.

Endnotes

Chapter One: Our Men in Madagascar

1. U.S. Department of State, D557, https://catalog.archives.gov/id/211474478.
2. See Charles Stuart Kennedy, *The American Consul: A History of the United States Consular Service 1776–1924*, rev. 2nd ed., (Washington, DC: New Academia, 2015), especially chapters 1 and 2, for a thorough review of the early history of consuls.
3. Palfrey never made it to Paris, dying at sea in 1780. The first American to perish abroad in the diplomatic service of his country, Palfrey's name is thirty-three spaces before Stanwood's on the memorial to fallen diplomats maintained by the American Foreign Service Association in the lobby of the Harry S. Truman Building, the current headquarters of the Department of State.
4. Simeon Simeonov, "The Consular Caribbean: Consuls as Agents of Colonialism and Decolonisation in the Revolutionary Caribbean (1795–1848)," in *Memory, Migration and (De) Colonisation in the Caribbean and Beyond*, ed. Jack Webb, et al., (London: University of London Press), 122-123.
5. U.S. Department of State, D448, https://catalog.archives.gov/id/211473373.
6. Ibid., D380, https://catalog.archives.gov/id/211473882.
7. "Hova," originally the term for commoners in the Merina caste system, came to be used more frequently than "Merina" by foreigners to denote Madagascar's soldiers and, confusingly, sometimes even its ruling class. By Stanwood's era, the term was used to generally mean the government in Antananarivo.
8. U.S. Department of State, D207, https://catalog.archives.gov/id/211473882.
9. Lambert himself had retired to the Comoros in 1865, but a company representing his interests continued to operate in Madagascar after his departure.
10. U.S. Department of State, D234, https://catalog.archives.gov/id/211472816.
11. A Former Resident of the Island, *Madagascar and the United States* (New York: Thompson and Moreau Printers, 1883).
12. "Treaty of Commerce and Navigation Between The United States and Madagascar," signed at Antananarivo, February 14, 1867; modified in Washington, D.C., in 1883.
13. Gwyn Campbell, "Madagascar and the Slave Trade, 1810-1895," *The Journal of African History* 22, no. 2 (1981): 217, http://www.jstor.org/stable/181583.
14. U.S. Department of State, Microfiche 121, https://catalog.archives.gov/id/211474478.
15. Andakabe despatch, number unknown, June 7, 1888. NOTE: Stanwood's despatches do not appear to be recorded in the National Archives, except indirectly through duplicates in the Tamatave despatches and other federal records. For example, this message is reproduced in a report from the Executive to Congress following Stanwood's death: "Presidential message on affairs in Madagascar." U.S. Congressional Serial Set, 1888.

Chapter Two: Baron Duverge

1. *New York Times*, "Captain Duverge's Career," December 24, 1888.
2. *Allen's Indian Mail*, June 5, 1863, 486.
3. An interesting coincidence is that the similarly named *Sphinx* was commissioned in Duverge's ancestral home of Bordeaux in 1863, the same year of the *Sphynx*'s disappearance on the other side of the world. The French *Sphinx*, though, unlike the modest commercial schooner that vanished off of Colombo, was a 165-foot, copper-bottomed ironclad that had been covertly ordered by the Confederacy to break the Union blockade. Its eventual fate was just as unique as the ship on which Duverge had

sailed. The name "Sphinx" was selected to suggest that the warship was actually destined for the Egyptian Navy, as sale to the Rebels would have been against French law. American diplomats became aware of the ironclad's true owners and pressured France to instead sell the vessel to Denmark. The Danes, however, sold the *Sphinx* to the Confederacy, who christened her the CSS *Stonewall*. After a circuitous voyage around Europe and then across the Atlantic, the *Stonewall* arrived in Cuba in November 1865. The war then being concluded, she was handed over to the Union Navy. From there, the *Sphinx* sailed to Washington, D.C. It is highly likely that Duverge, a career mariner and student of naval warfare, would have taken note of the other *Sphinx* during this time, when he himself was soldiering along the Atlantic coast.

4. *Allen's Indian Mail,* August 1, 1863.

5. *Sphynx,* 5057 Admiralty Court Instances London, 1859, Folio 5057.

6. Gerard's letter offers that Duverge "*a reçu une bonne* éducation *à Bordeaux*." St. Helena, no. unknown. August 9, 1864, https://catalog.archives.gov/id/212183980.

7. It is notable that nearly 30% of U.S. Army officers left service at the start of the Civil War to join the Confederacy. Elden E. Billings, "The Civil War and Conscription," *Current History* 54, no. 322 (June 1968): 333–366, http://www.jstor.org/stable/45311920.

8. Thomas J. Ward Jr., "ENEMY COMBATANTS: Black Soldiers in Confederate Prisons," *Army History* 78 (Winter 2011): 32–41, http://www.jstor.org/stable/26298931.

9. "The Life of Henry Warren Howe: Consisting of Diary and Letters," Lowell, MA. Privately printed.

10. Approximately one in three Northern soldiers were immigrants like Agnus and Duverge. There were comparatively few foreign-born participants on the side of the Confederacy.

11. Rossiter Johnson and John Howard Brown, *The Twentieth Century Biographical Dictionary of Notable Americans* (Boston: The Biographical Society, 1904), 63-64.

12. Brian Matthew Jordan, "'Our Work Is Not Yet Finished': Union Veterans and Their Unending Civil War, 1865–1872," *Journal of the Civil War Era* 5, no. 4 (December 2015): 484–503, http://www.jstor.org/stable/26070350.

13. Henry Warren Howe, diary, 202.

14. David Power Conyngham, *Soldiers of the Cross, the Authoritative Text: The Heroism of Catholic Chaplains and Sisters in the American Civil War*, annotated edition, ed. David J. Endres and William B. Kurtz (Notre Dame: University of Notre Dame Press, May 30, 2019), 342.

15. Samuel Pasfield Oliver, *Madagascar: An Historical and Descriptive Account of the Island and its Former Dependencies, Volume 1* (New York: Macmillan, 1886), 94.

Chapter Three: Duverge the Adventurer

1. *New York Times,* October 29, 1881.

2. *Baltimore Sun,* December 1881.

3. *Washington Evening Star,* February 8, 1882.

4. Act of August 15, 1856, 11 Statutes at large, "An Act to Regulate the Diplomatic and Consular Systems."

5. Mary H. Kingsley, *Travels in West Africa: Congo Français, Corisco, and Cameroons* (London: Macmillan, 1897). There is no record of Kingsley meeting Duverge, though she did have some interaction with Vice-Consul Newton's trading firm, which she characterized as "English," perhaps because his partner was English or maybe because of Newton's status as the British consul.

6. St. Paul de Loanda no. X, Microfice 5, November 12, https://catalog.archives.gov/id/212190040.

7. See Gwyn Campbell, "Madagascar and the Slave Trade, 1810-1895," *The Journal of African History* 22, no. 2 (1981): http://www.jstor.org/stable/181583, which cites Duverge's reporting for insights into Angola's evolving economy in the 1880s.

8. Duverge annual commerce report.

9. St. Paul de Loanda no. X, Microfice 30, November 12, https://catalog.archives.gov/id/212190040.

10. Ibid., Microfice 26, November 10, 1882, https://catalog.archives.gov/id/212190040.

11. Ibid., Microfice 67, https://catalog.archives.gov/id/212190040.

12. U.S. Department of State, D100, https://catalog.archives.gov/id/212190040.

13. Ibid., Whether or not she brought with her to America the young "specimen of slave traffic in Africa" is unknown; no further mention of the child appears in the historical record.

14. The first of these associations, the International African Association (the AIA, in French) lasted until 1879, when it was replaced by the confusingly similarly named International Association of the Congo. To further confuse matters, Leopold and his proxies attempted to obfuscate their true goals by using stationery and titles from the different associations interchangeably when interacting with local chiefs. To keep matters simple, all Leopold-sponsored activity during this period will be referred to as having originated from the "association," understanding that different legal entities with varying authorities existed during different times.

15. Tim Jeal, *Stanley: The Impossible Life of Africa's Greatest Adventure* (New Haven: Yale University Press, 2008), 163.

16. Jeal, quoting Stanwood to Edward Levy-Lawson, August 17, 1877, 214.

17. Jeal, 243.

18. The Kabindas, a tribal group from the interior of Congo, did not originate from "Cabinda," the present-day Angolan exclave situated along the Atlantic Coast, but from a region further west in what is today the Democratic Republic of the Congo.

19. Congo Free State Volume 1, 490.

20. Congo Free State Founding, Stanley, 52.

21. Académie Royale des Sciences d'Outre-Mer, "Verge (Du)," https://www.kaowarsom.be/fr/notices_verge_du.

22. Shaw Stanley letter, 1.

23. Adolphe Burdo, "Le Congo et ses affluents, publié sous la direction de Ch. de Martrin-Donos," in *Les Belges dans l'Afrique Centrale: Voyages, Aventures, et Découvertes* (Belgium: P. Maes, 1890), 468-469.

24. Henry Morton Stanley, *The Congo and the Founding of its Free State: A Story of Work and Exploration*, 2 vols (1886), 248.

25. C. 1014-1, Stanley's letters from the Museum of Central Africa.

26. *The Guardian* (London, Greater London, England), December 15, 1883, 9.

27. Henry Morton Stanley, *The Congo and the Founding of its Free State: A Story of Work and Exploration*, 2 vols. (1886), 273-274.

28. Henry Phillips, "An Account of the Congo Independent State," *Proceedings of the American Philosophical Society* 26, no. 130 (1889): 459–76, http://www.jstor.org/stable/983184.

29. Alexis-Marie Gochet, *Le Congo belge illustré: ou l'état indépendant du Congo sous la souveraineté de s. m. Léopold II, roi des Belges* (Belgium: H. Dessain, 1887), 183.

30. His activities resulted in the United States Consul General in Lisbon being summoned by the Portuguese Foreign Minister. Diplomatic Correspondence, Portugal, Vol. XXXI, No. 95 (Confidential), Francis to Frelinghuysen, November 23, 1883.

31. The State Department did not forget the incident, though. A decade later, Consul Downing requested funding to visit Congo once per year to examine "trespasses against U.S. citizens in the Upper Congo"; the request was denied. Brian Russell Roberts, *Artistic Ambassadors: Literary and International Representation of the New Negro Era* (United Kingdom: University of Virginia Press, 2013), 82.

32. Antoine Perraud, *Escape from Madagascar: Journals of a French Marine, 1884-1887*, trans. Marilyn O'Day (self-published, 2002), 131.

Chapter Four: The Cemetery of Europeans

1. *The New York Times*, "Lois Leopold du Rothier Du Verge's Wife Tired of Him," March 12, 1885.

2. U.S. Department of State, D246, https://catalog.archives.gov/id/211473882.

3. Ibid., D247, https://catalog.archives.gov/id/211473882.

4. Ibid., D297, https://catalog.archives.gov/id/211473882.

5. Coincidentally, Oliver was present at the 1862 coronation of Radama II of Madagascar as a member of the British delegation. This is the event Duverge likely attended according to his 1865 letter to President Johnson.

6. Samuel Pasfield Oliver, *The True Story of the French Dispute in Madagascar* (London: T. Fisher Unwin, 1885), 242.

7. While Antananarivo was the Hova capital, many states situated their diplomatic presence in Tamatave. Not only was the port city more accessible, it allowed representatives to play neutral

in the conflict between the French and the Hovas. The American consul in 1883, for instance, was instructed by Secretary of State Frelinghuysen that the "temporary intermission of your relations with the Madagascarian authorities in Tamatave does not exempt you from the moral obligation as a representative of the Govt of the United States to use your good office for the protection of American citizens and property within your jurisdictional limits and that in case anything should occur calling for your intervention you will feel it your duty to address yourself to whatever authority may be in responsible administrative control of the port." (Secretary of State Frelinghuysen to Whitney, 108 MS inst consuls, 185.)

8. Antoine Perraud, *Escape from Madagascar: Journals of a French Marine, 1884-1887*, trans. Marilyn O'Day (self-published, 2002), 68.

9. It was in this note that Duverve included his almost certainly false claim that he had fought in the Anglo-Ashanti War of 1873.

10. Marked "325" in Malagasy State Archives, letter from Duverge to PM, October 8, 1884, 1.

11. "French Aggression in Madagascar," *The Fortnightly Review*, vol. XLVII (January 1–June 1, 1887): 437.

12. Perraud, 65.

13. Ibid., 70.

14. Ibid., 60.

15. Bako, Malagasy Official Archives letter, June 5, 1885, 45.

16. Perraud, 64.

17. Samuel Pasfield Oliver, *Madagascar: An Historical and Descriptive Account of the Island and Its Former Dependencies* (United Kingdom: Macmillan, 1886), 172.

18. U.S. Department of State, D330, https://catalog.archives.gov/id/211473882.

19. Bako, Malagasy Official Archives letter, March 20, 1885.

20. U.S. Department of State, D146, https://catalog.archives.gov/id/211473882.

21. Ibid., D391, https://catalog.archives.gov/id/211473882.

22. The Orders and Medals Research Society, Spring 1982, 49.

23. Bako, Malagasy Official Archives letter, August 27, 1885, 32.

24. Ibid., November 30, 1885, 42.

25. Ibid., December 2, 1885, 44.

26. U.S. Department of State, D177, https://catalog.archives.gov/id/211474478.

27. Ibid., D209, https://catalog.archives.gov/id/211474478.

28. Louis Duverge, *Madagascar et Peuplades Indépendantes: Abandonnées par la France*, ed. Challamel Ainé (Paris: Libraire Algérienne et Coloniale, 1887).

29. Ibid., 18.

30. Ibid., 8.

31. Ibid., 78.

32. Ibid., 27.

33. Ibid., 67.

34. Ibid., 65.

35. Ibid., 131.

36. Mike Parker Pearson and Karen Godden, *In Search of the Red Slave: Shipwreck and Captivity in Madagascar* (United Kingdom: Sutton, 2002), 121.

37. Duverge, 58.

38. Ibid., 4.

39. Ibid., 64.

40. Ibid., 161.

41. Perraud, 56.

Chapter Five: Death in Boston

1. "Colonel L R Du Verge: A Hero of Many Scrapes that Make the Story of His Life a Romantic One," *Boston Globe*, February 28, 1886.

2. Antoine Perraud, *Escape from Madagascar: Journals of a French Marine, 1884-1887*, trans. Marilyn O'Day (self-published, 2002), 61.

3. *Boston Globe*, May 20 1887.

4. Ibid., May 23, 1887.

5. This child was very likely the second of four children Duverge fathered. The first was a boy, recorded as born in Devon in 1872 to an unknown mother. It is possible the child was born at sea. The parish where the birth was recorded, Stoke Damerel, was a frequent port of entry for vessels arriving from America. Duverge would have two more boys in later life, both of whom died as infants.

6. Henry G. Tricket met a fate similar to that of the Marquis. After publishing a highly inaccurate account of the Lizzie Borden case in 1892, he faced charges in Massachusetts for bribery of police sources. While a fugitive aboard a train in Canada, he slipped between railcars and fell to an instant death. See Edwin H. Porter, *The Fall River Tragedy: A History of the Borden Murders*, Chapter XI for details of Borden defamation. Ticker's death is recorded in "Henry G Trickey's Death," *New York Times*, December 6, 1892.

7. Perraud, 117.

8. Ibid., 134.

9. Ibid., 134.

10. Ibid., 143.

11. Ibid., 143.

12. Ibid., 8.

13. Affairs in Madagascar Report to Congress from State Department, Consul Campbell letter, 9.

14. Madagascar Report, 77.

15. U.S. Department of State, D503, https://catalog.archives.gov/id/211473882.

16. Ibid., D408, https://catalog.archives.gov/id/211473373.

17. "Washington County classifieds," *Portland Daily Press*, November 17, 1882.

18. U.S. Department of State, D114, https://catalog.archives.gov/id/211475150.

19. Ibid., D317, https://catalog.archives.gov/id/211475150.

20. Ibid., D378, https://catalog.archives.gov/id/211475150.

Chapter Six: Stanwood of the West Coast

1. U.S. Department of State, D142, https://catalog.archives.gov/id/211475150.

2. *New South Wales Police Gazette*, November 12, 1879, 422.

3. U.S. Department of State, D35, https://catalog.archives.gov/id/211473373.

4. Ibid., D67, https://catalog.archives.gov/id/211473373.

5. Ibid., D35, https://catalog.archives.gov/id/211473373.

6. Ibid., D61, https://catalog.archives.gov/id/211473373.

7. Ibid., D153, https://catalog.archives.gov/id/211473373.

8. Ibid., D205, https://catalog.archives.gov/id/211473882.

9. Ibid., D170, https://catalog.archives.gov/id/211473882

10. Ibid., D191, https://catalog.archives.gov/id/211473882.

11. Ibid., D122, https://catalog.archives.gov/id/211473882.

12. Ibid., D207, https://catalog.archives.gov/id/211473882.

13. Ibid., D174, https://catalog.archives.gov/id/211473882.

14. Ibid., D84, https://catalog.archives.gov/id/211473882.

15. Ibid., D102, https://catalog.archives.gov/id/211473882.

16. Ibid., D448, https://catalog.archives.gov/id/211473882.

17. Ibid., D162, https://catalog.archives.gov/id/211473882.

18. Ibid., D431, https://catalog.archives.gov/id/211473882.

19. Consular reports, v. 10, July–Oct. 1883, nos. 31–34; special report on declared exports for U.S., 1st and 2nd quarters of 1883, I (1883), 11.

20. British and Foreign State Papers, 1879–1880, LXXL, 513.

21. U.S. Department of State, D285, https://catalog.archives.gov/id/211473882.

22. Gwyn Campbell, "Madagascar and the Slave Trade, 1810-1895," *The Journal of African History* 22, no. 2 (1981): 222, http://www.jstor.org/stable/181583.

23. U.S. Department of State, D257, https://catalog.archives.gov/id/211474478.

24. Ibid., D285, https://catalog.archives.gov/id/211473882.

25. Ibid., D410, https://catalog.archives.gov/id/211475150.

26. Ibid., D411, https://catalog.archives.gov/id/211475150.

27. Ibid., D102–109, https://catalog.archives.gov/id/211473882.

28. Ibid., D112, https://catalog.archives.gov/id/211473882.

29. State Department Press Release, September 19, 1931.

30. *Overtime in Heaven* is an extraordinary text written by two of the most esteemed journalists of their era. The book's forward was written by Secretary of State Dean Rusk. The epilogue was supposed to be the text of a speech that President Kennedy gave to members of the Foreign Service. Kennedy approved the speech's inclusion in the book but was assassinated before he could approve a final declassified version. Ultimately his brother, Attorney General Robert Kennedy, cleared on the book's epilogue.

31. Peter Lisagor and Marguerite Higgins, *Overtime in Heaven* (New York: Doubleday, 1964), 58.

32. Campbell, 206.

33. U.S. Department of State, D524, https://catalog.archives.gov/id/211475150.

34. Ibid., D470, https://catalog.archives.gov/id/211474478.

35. Ibid., D92, https://catalog.archives.gov/id/211475150.

36. Ibid., D123, https://catalog.archives.gov/id/211475150.

37. Ibid., D500, https://catalog.archives.gov/id/211473882.

38. Ibid., D479, https://catalog.archives.gov/id/211474478.

39. Ibid., D485, https://catalog.archives.gov/id/211474478.

40. Ibid., D192, https://catalog.archives.gov/id/211474478.

41. "The Quarrel in Madagascar, *New York Times*, October 6, 1887.

Chapter Seven: Murder in Belo

1. U.S. Department of State, D492, https://catalog.archives.gov/id/211474478.

2. Ibid., D502, https://catalog.archives.gov/id/211474478.

3. McDade testimony.

4. "Nosy" is the Malagasy word for "island." Nosy Ve, a desolated scrap of land that was also called "Sandy Island" by Duverge, should not be confused with Nosy Be in the country's north, today a popular tourist destination for local and foreign visitors. While it is possible Duverge anchored off the island of Nosy Ve, this and subsequent references to the location, occasionally misspelled "Nosy Vey" or "Nosy Vy" in some records, likely refer to activity along the coastline, which was more significantly populated.

5. U.S. Department of State, D611, https://catalog.archives.gov/id/211474478.

6. Captain McGowna, ship log, USS *Swatara*.

7. USS *Swatara* report.

8. U.S. Department of State, D66, https://catalog.archives.gov/id/153389401.

9. Ibid., D551, https://catalog.archives.gov/id/211474478.

10. Ibid., D109, https://catalog.archives.gov/id/211475150.

11. Ibid., D577, https://catalog.archives.gov/id/211474478.

12. Ibid., D385, https://catalog.archives.gov/id/211475150.

13. Ibid., D555, https://catalog.archives.gov/id/211474478.

14. Ibid., D549, https://catalog.archives.gov/id/211474478.

15. Bako, Malagasy Official Archives letter, December 17, 1888, 98.

16. U.S. Department of State, D555, https://catalog.archives.gov/id/211474478.

17. Ibid., D591, https://catalog.archives.gov/id/211474478.

18. Ibid., D141, https://catalog.archives.gov/id/211475150.

19. Ibid., D496, https://catalog.archives.gov/id/211474478.

Chapter Eight: The Trial of Duverge

1. Cong. Rec., 50th Cong., 2d sess., March 1, 1889, Ex Doc: 166.

2. U.S. Department of State, D151, https://catalog.archives.gov/id/211475150.

3. Ibid., D102, https://catalog.archives.gov/id/169795564.

4. Ibid., D66, https://catalog.archives.gov/id/153389401.

5. In Re Ross, 140 US 453.

6. W.W. Robinson to W. Hunter, July 15, 1879, No. 46; USCD, Tam.

7. U.S. Department of State, D103, https://catalog.archives.gov/id/211475150.

8. Ibid., D165, https://catalog.archives.gov/id/211475150.

9. Ibid., D170, https://catalog.archives.gov/id/211475150.

10. Middleton was correct. The moon above Belo on November 5, 1888, was a waxing crescent; fewer than four-percent of the light regularly reflected from the moon was visible that evening.

11. U.S. Department of State, D263, https://catalog.archives.gov/id/211475150.

12. Ibid., D283, https://catalog.archives.gov/id/211475150.

13. Ibid., D322, https://catalog.archives.gov/id/211475150.

14. Ibid., D330, https://catalog.archives.gov/id/211475150.

15. U.S. Consular Regulations for 1888, 215, Sec 596.

16. U.S. Department of State, D118, https://catalog.archives.gov/id/211475150.

17. Ibid., D106, https://catalog.archives.gov/id/211475150.

18. Ibid., D155, https://catalog.archives.gov/id/169795564.

Chapter Nine: The Unwanted Prisoner

1. Crawford M. Bishop, "The American Consular Court System in China," *American Bar Association Journal* 8, no. 4 (1922): 223–25, http://www.jstor.org/stable/25710855.

2. John Bassett Moore, *Digest of International Law*, vol. 2, U.S. Congressional Serial Set (1900): i-1124, 637.

3. Anson Burlingame, "Mr. Burlingame to Mr. Seward," June 3, 1864, Office of the Historian, https://history.state.gov/historicaldocuments/frus1864p3/d420.

4. U.S. Department of State, D404, https://catalog.archives.gov/id/211475150.

5. Ibid., D410, https://catalog.archives.gov/id/211475150.

6. Ibid., D550, https://catalog.archives.gov/id/211475150.

7. Ibid., D551, https://catalog.archives.gov/id/211475150.

8. Moore, 635.

9. U.S. Department of State, D419, https://catalog.archives.gov/id/211475150.

10. Ibid., D108, https://catalog.archives.gov/id/211475150.

11. Ibid., D476, https://catalog.archives.gov/id/211475150.

12. Ibid., D478, https://catalog.archives.gov/id/211475150.

13. Ibid., D496, https://catalog.archives.gov/id/211475150.

14. Ibid., D12, https://catalog.archives.gov/id/211475150.

15. Ibid., D475, https://catalog.archives.gov/id/211475150.

16. Ibid., D40, https://catalog.archives.gov/id/211475150.

17. Ibid., D141, https://catalog.archives.gov/id/211475150.

18. Ibid., D244, https://catalog.archives.gov/id/211475150.

19. Ibid., D245, https://catalog.archives.gov/id/211475150.

20. J. A Holder, *Among the Malagasy, An Unconventional Record of Missionary Experience* (London, James Clark Publisher, 1912), 260-261.

21. U.S. Department of State, D284, https://catalog.archives.gov/id/211475150.

Chapter Ten: The End of the Century

1. Andriamanantena later moved to New York, shortened his name to "Paul Razaf," and became a composer, gaining fame writing lyrics for the Big Band standards "Ain't Misbehavin'" and "In the Mood."

2. Phares M. Mutibwa, "Primary Resistance Against the French in Madagascar, 1895–1900" *Transafrican Journal of History* 8, no. 1/2 (1979): 105–13, http://www.jstor.org/stable/24328506.

3. U.S. Department of State, D128, https://catalog.archives.gov/id/211477035.

4. Randall Bennett Woods, *A Black Odyssey: John Lewis Waller and the Promise of American Life* (Lawrence: University Press of Kansas, 2021), 131–139.

5. Liliana Mosca, "The Merina Kingdom in the Late 1870s as Reported in the Despatches of Colonel William W. Robinson, U.S. Consul in Madagascar," 126, http://madarevues.recherches.gov.mg/IMG/pdf/omaly37-40_8_-2.pdf.

About the Author

Nick Pietrowicz spent twenty-three years as a special agent with the State Department's Diplomatic Security Service. Joining immediately after 9/11, his first tour to the New York Field Office was abbreviated when he volunteered to go to Port au Prince, Haiti. There, he protected the American Embassy and its staff following the collapse of President Aristide's government and the ensuing period of anarchy. Nick was then posted to the Miami Field Office, curtailing to volunteer for service in Kabul, Afghanistan. Arriving in the summer of 2006, he spent a year on the ambassador's protective detail while simultaneously managing the embassy's guard force. Nick was then assigned to Moldova, his first tour as an embassy chief of security, where he led an investigation into one of the largest nuclear material smuggling cases in the country's history. Nick followed this with an assignment to Chad, where he killed a black mamba with a can of WD-40 and handed out Chick-fil-A sauce on the Libyan border. His next overseas tour was to Luanda, Angola, which included substantial travel throughout the country and the rest of Africa. His most recent overseas tours were in Australia and then Bosnia and Herzegovina. He now works in Washington, D.C., where he never misses an episode of *Jeopardy*.

www.ingramcontent.com/pod-product-compliance
Lightning Source LLC
Chambersburg PA
CBHW011200090426
42740CB00020B/3415